Lessons
Book II

By Alex
Through Michelle Wedel

Edited by: Paul Wedel

Sweetgrass Press L.L.C.
P.O. Box 1862
Merrimack, NH 03054

Michelle LaVigne-Wedel. 1962-

Library of Congress Control Number: 2007902816

Lessons Book II / Through Michelle Wedel
with Alex

10 Digit ISBN 0-9745434-9-7
13 Digit ISBN 978-0-9745434-9-9

COVER DESIGN: The Electric Wigwam
Cover Photo : The Cat's Eye Nebula
Credit: NASA, ESA, HEIC, and The Hubble Heritage Team
(STScI/AURA)

Printed in the United States of America

Address all inquiries:
Sweetgrass Press L.L.C.
P.O. Box 1862
Merrimack, NH 03054-1862

Please visit www.sweetgrasspress.com for more information.

Table of Contents

Important Note

In *Lessons Book II*, Alex relies heavily on the assumption that the reader has read and has a basic understanding of the concepts in the original book, *Lessons*. Though some concepts from the first book are reviewed in this volume, it is highly recommended that you read the original book, *Lessons*, before reading *Lessons Book II*.

Foreword

Teacher, guide, confidant, and friend are all words I use freely and with pride when describing the author of the book you now hold in your hands. In the many years that I have had the honor to know Alex, I have been humbled by his wisdom, humility, and compassion. He is a "man" like no other, for, indeed, he is not a man, but a spirit being and master. His truth is his reality and everything in him supersedes what I would call human, for no human I have ever known has exercised the discipline and compassion that Alex has demonstrated when his spirit was channeled through my wife, Michelle.

Michelle Wedel, whose hands typed the words in this book, used her tremendous gift of the ability to full body channel to provide Alex with the vehicle to present his teachings with a clarity, conciseness, and accuracy of content that would not have otherwise been possible. As Michelle and I read through the manuscript of Lessons Book II, we were continually taken aback by Alex's uniquely fresh views and information about the earth, the spirit world, and Creation itself.

Lessons Book II is an astonishing look at the nature of the human soul on earth, the spirit world outside of physical existence, and the grand scope of an eternal Creation. Alex's componential analysis of the most complex, enigmatic mysteries of the human condition translates into a comprehensive and understandable model that challenges the reader to reconsider his view of the universe. It is a journey that leads the reader through wide valleys of thought, up steep paradigmatic cliffs, and onto a plane of realization that compels the reader to expand his view of the universe's construction.

Our period in history demands a striking spiritual statement be made in the face of the tsunamic technological growth that overwhelms our senses daily. I believe Lessons Book II represents such a statement because it is a tome whose field of vision stretches from a prodigious, eternal Creation, to the comparatively microscopic existence of humankind. It is a book whose time has come.

Paul Wedel
April 23, 2007

Before We Begin

Dear one, once again we come together to bring you the keys to unlock the tools you need to do your world's work. Before I begin to impart new information and concepts, I feel it is a good thing to briefly review some of the concepts you have already been presented in previous lessons. Each of these concepts is important and will be used as a basis for the new concepts about to be set before you.

First, remember as you read the pages that follow, many times the information given will agree with your preconceived concepts and what you have been told by other sources and other teachers. Be aware that this may not always be the case. Some, maybe even much of the information contained herein, could be very different or even contrary to things you already know and believe. Let me remind you, it does not automatically mean that the information you know or that which is contained in these lessons is faulty or untrue. It simply means that the different teachers presenting information to you have different pieces of truth to offer you. Often, if you look closely at the different pieces of information, you will see they are just different views of the same concept. One view may be tailored to fit one situation or audience, while the other is presented from a different point of reference. Nevertheless, they are the same ultimate truths.

Of course, there will be times when information you receive from different sources clashes totally and it becomes clear that one or the other has to be faulty. In this case, I caution you not to focus on the source of the information, but rather to focus on what the information does when applied to your heart song. If something rings true to you and you can feel it in your heart, then believe it. If the information does not fit in your personal toolbox and you find yourself struggling to believe it, then let it drop. This is true if the source of the information is a child, a neighbor, a Ph.D., or a channeled spirit.

This brings me to my second point. Beyond anything you will ever read anywhere; beyond anything that any person or spirit can tell or teach you; comes your own personal truth. What is truth to you is ultimately what you will use to base your life and life's work on. Your mission must be directed and measured by your own understanding of what is true to you. Do not let anyone's comments such as, "My sources have told me that you are going to be a healer," or "The spirit I channel says you have to go to Tibet in order to find your own truth," make you do anything that is not in your heart already. Take such things as suggestions only, then apply your own personal knowledge and understanding of your mission to them to see if they sing to your heart. If they do, then pursue them. But if they do not, do not waste time with them. Know, child, that truth will remain truth. Have no fear that you will disregard an important truth by listening to your heart. If the truth presented to you is important to your growth or your work, it will become apparent to you in time. Indeed, it will become apparent to you at the proper time, when you need it. So be true to yourself no matter what others say.

That said, let me remind you about the art of learning itself. If you recall from the first book of lessons, child, you are a complete being. You are a perfect reflection of eternity. Being so, you are whole. You lack nothing, not even knowledge. Therefore, the art of learning, for you, is simply the art of remembering and becoming aware of what you already know. This is why it is important that all truths you have doubts about be tested against your inner voice. The correct answer is in you. Does the piece you are holding match it?

Always be mindful that you are not learning anything. You are simply becoming aware of things you already know in a higher state. Unfortunately, your present physical form does not let you have access to all your knowledge at one time. You can, however, access that knowledge in bits and pieces as needed. You can also activate dormant knowledge that you hold inside yourself. The activation of dormant knowledge is what you have come to know as learning.

Not everything you learn in this earth-life that applies as a truth on the physical plane is actually a universal truth. Recall, child, your earth-life is merely an illusion you have covered yourself in. This earth is a node in the mesh of the universe that is undergoing friction and strife, thus causing struggle that must be overcome in order for Creation to learn and grown. In order to help this effort, you have separated a part of yourself from the total oneness of Creation and have taken on this illusion. Though we talked about the illusion of physical life in some detail in the first book of lessons, we will review the basic principles of true reality at this time.

Remember, only things eternal are truly real. Everything that is eternal is constantly in a state of growth. If it were not growing and changing, it would have an end. Things that end are not eternal, and therefore, not part of true reality.

Let us review the six basic principles of true reality and all things eternal in it. That is, of course, all things truly real and not just illusion.

1) The true universe, that which is more than the physical universe of stars and planets, has no beginning or ending in any direction of time, space, or dimension. Eternity, as we discussed before, is not just an unending linear timeline. It is the total of all things that exist. It never began and will never end. If you walked for all your existence in one straight line from the center, (which, of course, would be for all existence since you are eternal), you would never approach a boarder or outer ring of eternity. In fact, you would always be in the center.

2) If something has an ending, it also has a beginning. Remember, this is important when you are trying to decide if something is real or merely illusion. If you can look at something and say to yourself, "This is complete and unchanging. This is ended," then it had a beginning somewhere.

Therefore, it is not eternal. Often, when we think of things, we fail to look at their beginnings or we cannot conceive of a time before they existed, therefore we miss the fact that they are merely illusions. But we can often easily conceive of the idea that those same things will someday end. If an ending can be found, any ending, not just in time, but in space, dimension, realm, vibration, or directions you have no names for, a beginning must be there as well. Likewise, if there is a beginning, then there will be an ending. You cannot be eternal in only one direction.

3) Since anything eternal encompasses all things, then it is reasonable to conclude that all things eternal are a total and perfect reflection of the greater eternity.

4) All things eternal are perfect and complete in their design. How can anything that is truly all things be incomplete? How can it be imperfect?

5) All things eternal have a complete and total opposite that is a complement to them. This complement is always completely and totally opposite in all ways. Yet, since it is itself eternal, it is completely and totally identical to its complement as well. This paradox is one in which volumes can be written.

6) The last concept I would like to remind you of is this; nothing eternal will ever remain the same. Everything that is real is constantly changing and growing. If it were not continually growing, it would have found an end to growth. If it found an end to anything, even growth, it would be illusion and not reality.

Be aware, child, that there are a few important things to be mindful of in these lessons that are addressed differently from how they were addressed in the lessons of the first book. That is because as your understanding grows, and the concepts become more complex to voice, the words we must use to describe these concepts have to grow as well. The most important difference you should be aware of is the use of the term "**dream**". In our first book of lessons together, "dream" referred to physical life and all else was inferred to be in true reality. As your understanding has grown, child, I am sure you have come to comprehend that spirits are still individual souls, yet true Creation is one unified source. This understanding is correct. Thus, you have come to know, or indeed, you have retrieved from your higher awareness, that there is a middle point between the dream and true Creation. That middle point MUST be within the dream.

So, what is this place where spirits live with greater understanding, and where your higher self resides? The answer, child, is that there are many layers of the dream. The closer you get to the physical, the deeper in the illusion you are. Spirits still live in the dream, but they know they are dreaming and are not limited to the physical illusion you and other embodied beings are. So, we will explore this set of lessons with the understanding that physical life is an **illusion** inside a **dream**. Everything that is in physical form will be considered in the illusion. Everything else is in the dream. That is, child, with the obvious exception of the Creation Force beyond the dream. To put it in simple terms, when you see references to the illusion, the reference infers physical things. When you see references to the dream, this infers the greater dream beyond that which is physical, but is still not united so totally with the Creation Force to be indistinguishable from it.

The next concept you will find more detailed in this book of lessons is the concept of frequency. In the first book, we explored frequencies in basic terms, handling complex concepts concerning frequencies of different types and functions, more or less as one concept. In this set of lessons, our exploration of frequencies will bring us further into the world of vibration and tone and will introduce and explain the many different types of frequency manifestations, their origins, and how to work with them.

So, child, please keep in mind the difference between the illusion, the dream, and true reality, as well as the concept that there are many types of frequencies. Otherwise, you could find yourself missing important concepts that will be presented within these parameters.

These things said, and fresh in your mind, let us continue with our lessons.

Lesson 1
The Word is Thought

I am sure you have heard it said, "I think, therefore I am". Could it be the truth that just by the simple act of knowing that you have thought, you become alive? Could it be that the shear awareness of life creates life? Or, could it be that the thought itself is life?

When you assess your state of being and say to yourself, "I am alive," what do you use as a basis for your judgment? Is the mere ability to think about and question your own life proof that you are? Is life measured by one's ability to comprehend its existence?

The answers to these questions may seem simple and inclusive in the statement, "I think, therefore I am". But, child, I must tell you that the power of the statement, "I think, therefore I am", lies not in the ability to think, but in the thought itself. Let us explore this statement from a viewpoint not limited to physical reality, thus, finding how profound these words actually are.

When you apply the laws that govern things eternal to your physical life, you will see that your physical life is merely illusion. You were born, therefore your physical life began. And when you die, your physical life will end. If during this time you think, thus believe, you are alive, you are wrong. But

I must tell you, child, that if you think and thus *know* you are alive, then you are.

You may be wondering what the difference is? To believe that you are a living, conscious part of Creation because you *can* think is wrong. This is because it applies limits to a limitless concept. In fact, child, you are alive because you *are* thought. In fact, thought is all you really are. All you feel in an emotional sense, all you think with logic, reason, intuition, or faith, all you know, all you believe, your personality, your sense of humor, your eye for beauty, and anything else that is a function of your soul is contained in the substance that you are. You are thought. Thought is energy in a pattern. The pattern that energy takes is thought. Thought is you.

From the moment you enter this dream, you begin to think. It may seem like an odd question, but how do you know you are thinking? When you examine how you think, you will likely find that your thoughts manifest in two distinct ways. The first is conceptual thought.

Conceptual thought is made up of feelings, emotions, and concepts you experience on a primal level. That is, these thoughts are experienced without words. No inner voice echoes in your head saying, "I am sad. I am happy," etc. You simply experience these things without words, unless you take the time to apply the second manifestation of thought to the otherwise wordless concept.

The second type of thought is that of worded thought. This is what you, child, are more likely to call thought in the first place. This type of thought is always accompanied by words. Regardless of the language you speak, these thoughts will run through your brain in a stream of recognizable words.

Take a moment and think. Think about anything. Ponder the room you are in, the book in your hands, or anything else that comes to mind. Pay attention to how you are thinking. You will find that unless you have been working and practicing very intensely at developing conceptual thinking, it is likely that you will find it near to impossible to focus your thoughts on any physical thing without your mind automatically applying words to your thoughts.

Just like your soul has adapted to fit your body — your tool kit — the energy that is your soul has developed a way to communicate with your dreaming self. It does this by applying recognizable words to the energy of the concepts that it is experiencing at the time. Or rather, child, the you that is your higher self — the you that is beyond the limits of the physical illusion — is sending the you that is lost in the illusion clues, hints, and directions in a form that is easily interpreted in the illusion.

Remember child, physical life and all that is physically around you is an illusion constructed by Creation in order to grow. Also remember, all pieces of Creation, including your total self, are perfect and complete reflections of the greater Creation, or of God.

In the Bible, in John 1:1, it says, *"In the beginning was the Word, and the Word was with God, and the Word was God."* Knowing what you now know about the origin of thought, let us explore this biblical verse and see if we can find the profound meaning the author intended. It is often believed, and generally accepted, that *"the word"* as given in this verse of the Bible refers to one person, that person being Christ. But this interpretation is merely a convenient attempt at explaining something misunderstood in a way comfortable to the dogma of the reader. In fact, the true explanation makes far more sense. Look at the verse again. *"In the beginning was the Word, and the Word was with God, and the Word was God."* Indeed, *"the word"* referred to in this verse refers to all, for *"the word"* is thought. In the above case, it is clearly the thought of God. But look carefully, child, who came first? If we are to believe the verse above, it is clear that *"the word"* existed before God did.

Could it be that God thought, therefore God was? Clearly, this is what this verse says. And if that is so, then the verse above also makes it very clear that the word and God are one and the same. Thought is God. You are thought. Creation once again shows us that each eternal part is a perfect reflection of the greater whole.

You are alive in your thoughts. "I think, therefore I am," is true when applied to the thought that is "the word".

We can prove the power of words and thoughts and even examine how they are one and the same when we look at how they affect the illusion. Simply by its very presence and invocation, thought can change what you perceive as physical reality. It can build quicker than any hammer and kill more efficiently than any knife. It is also said, and I am sure you have heard, *"The pen is mightier than the sword"*. Why is the pen mightier than the sword? Because, the pen is an agent of words. Words are thoughts in physical form. Thoughts are God.

Let us look at how easily and completely words affect thoughts and change the illusion. First, let us examine how this happens in small ways. You may wake in the morning feeling tired, but you are not feeling so ill that you are incapable of carrying on with your day. Early in the morning, you come across a friend or family member whose opinion you respect — in other words, somene whose words carry weight with — and he tells you that you look sick. He may even suggest that you need to lie down. His words enter your mind and become part of your thoughts, thus become part of your concept of physical reality. Those thoughts could easily create a reality scenario that reflects their content and you will become sicker. In most cases, you may not even know why the simple fatigue you had from the morning flared up into full illness by afternoon. You allowed your friend's words to affect your thoughts, and thus create your reality.

On a much larger scale, when many people listen to and allow the words of another to influence their thoughts, the combined power of their belief in the reality of those words and of the thoughts they inspire, can change the illusion which is physical reality in more substantial ways.

In the first set of lessons we discussed frequencies and how those of like frequencies band together for a common purpose. Those of like frequencies also have a tendency to maintain similar thought patterns. When those who hold similar thought patterns unite, particularly if their frequencies resonate favorably with each other, the illusion that is this physical world becomes susceptible to their consensus of thought. It is unfortunate, child, that by and large, those who do band together with both frequency and thought are generally those whose frequency is disturbed and not in proper focus. This creates "reality" problems. The consensus they create is that much more removed from what should exist. Fortunately, few in the above described situations realize the power in their hands, and fail to apply it to the fullest potential. Even fewer with positive direction realize the power for positive creation they could have if they banded together with like frequencies and thoughts.

To think is to be. To think in a positive direction is to be positive. If the bulk of a population thinks in a positive or negative direction, then most, if not all of the remainder will follow in suit, they will have to. Sometimes, these community attitudes are called nationalism. When a nation of people is focused on a common goal, a sense of belonging to that goal fills the people and they are fired up to reach that goal. Nothing is beyond their reach at this point. A world free from pain, starvation, hatred, and prejudice is possible. Great strides in medicine, social structure, and humanitarian efforts can be achieved with quick efficiency when the national spirit is invoked.

It is an unfortunate truth that most often this national spirit is invoked in the name of hatred and prejudice. Rather than uniting on a common good goal, humans, in general, tend to invoke nationalism in order to fight a common foe, usually creating a common foe in the process. War being the result.

More than just creating pain, war keeps the power out of the hands of the people. War keeps a population in poverty and fear. Moreover, it keeps a people focusing their creative energy and power on hatred of a common foe they are told is creating all their problems, rather than the true problem. That problem is always the frequency sickness of those who collect the power the people relinquish; be that a national leader, government, or religion.

Mankind's ability to create reality based on common thought has been used by those of negative influence for their own personal power since time first began. Why? Is it merely personal power those in control want?

The answer is no. No human benefits from the negative influence of the whole of mankind. Though those who try may see monetary gain, and may believe they are better off, the energy that makes up their full and higher selves suffer along with the rest of mankind. When they leave this life and return to the source, they will have to face the pain and suffering they caused. Not in the form of Biblical type eternal damnations, but something even more harsh. They will be all too aware of their true, dark motivations, and the evil influences they allowed to jade their decisions. This realization is beyond anyone's ability to explain to a mortal being. From the dream, it is hard for you to understand the different levels of suffering this will cause the souls of such persons when each returns to their higher self, but before they reunite with the total Creation Force.

In order to help those on earth understand it, some teachers have described it in human terms, trying to explain that the pain would be like the pain of a human body enduring eternal torture in a land of fire and brimstone. But I assure you this is a figurative explanation for the torment such a revelation will cause a person's higher being. That is, until they become aware on a higher level beyond the illusion they have chosen a negative path in order to be a mechanism of friction, thus helping the universe grow. For in true reality there is no distinction between good or evil, and when this being reunites with the Creation Force there is no punishment, for there was no true wrong committed. A paradox indeed.

Without evil actions, there would be nothing to cause the friction that good must struggle against to cause the growth of Creation. Yet, at the same time, by taking part in evil, these beings are stifling the growth of Creation. Since we are, each and every one, a perfect reflection of Creation, they are, in the purest truth, only hurting themselves. Yet, without their evil actions, Creation, and thus their own souls, would not grow, and therefore would no longer exist.

So, in a greater reality, good and evil are the same thing in that they perform the same function. They aid the growth of Creation. Nevertheless, in the world of earth-based reality, they are very different things. Thinking linearly, the one labeled good is preferable and beneficial to Creation. The other, labeled evil, is unwelcome and harmful to Creation. To have good prevail over evil is a common and very old concept of mankind. Yet, it is one that is not universal to individual humans.

Even those who prefer good can be heard to say, "Good guys finish last," and "Power can corrupt even the saint," and other sayings that perpetuate the myth that only through wickedness can a man become a success on Earth. Though this is not totally true, not even in the earth illusion, it is so commonly spoken that it is believed, and the consensus of those who believe it have made it appear to be so.

The world man has created is more than his buildings and his bridges. It is his thoughts and the concepts he agrees are true. It is also more. As you know from our first book of lessons, the Earth is about to go through a time of great change that can affect the balance of good and evil in all of physical creation. Because of this, the Earth and all who are on her and around her, are currently involved in a contest of sorts for the future direction of Creation. This struggle is being waged on many levels. Some levels are not physical. All are not real in the true greater sense of reality, as they are all taking place in different levels of the dream. The struggle is not fought with guns or other physical weapons, but with a much stronger force, thought. Paradoxically, in fact, in true reality, the game itself is already resolved and won by positive forces, as proven by your very existence. Yet, it will go on forever somewhere in the dream.

When we think of this struggle in the layers deeply set in the dream, where you are, child, we can see that it is more a game of wits and thought, than physical strife, for most of those involved. So, rather than labeling it a true struggle, battle, or war, it would be entirely appropriate to say it is a grand game of sorts. Thinking of what is unfolding around you with the term of "game" rather than "battle" has the advantage of focusing your thoughts in the correct direction.

It is unfortunate, child, there are those among you who fancy themselves to be spiritual warriors, emphasizing the perception that there is a need for violence as implied by the word 'warrior'. This gives validation to the concept that you are fighting a war. You are not. You are playing your part in the game of Creation. By limiting the concept to a war of good and evil, you remove any hope of enjoying your time playing the game. It is better to consider yourself a key player on the field, running with the ball towards the goal, and cleverly avoiding being tackled by other players, than a warrior running through your opponents with a sword, as you dodge one killing blow after another from a raging enemy bent on killing you. The analogy of a game is not only far more pleasant, but it is far more accurate. For indeed, child, you are playing the game that will bring about the growth of Creation. For the purpose of our lessons, we shall call this game the earth game.

The earth game has many levels of events unfolding with the help of many levels of beings that are paying attention to the game. Let us explore these different levels, the energies incarnate who make up the consensus of these levels, and how these things affect you and your mission on this earth.

Keep in mind as you read on, we will be exploring the levels of existence in the dream that you, child, from your current state of awareness, will be able to understand. When exploring any list of players or rules that apply to even this small part of the game plan of Creation, it is important that you are aware, child, that no printed book could ever list all the different varieties and motivations for all involved. For indeed, there are quite literally an eternity of options. So, keep in mind as you read forward, only the layers which are likely to touch you directly are to be explored in what we will call the earth game.

Lesson 2
The Earth Game

Before starting any explanation of the earth game, it is important to understand, child, that there are many levels to the dream, and many different ways of looking at things, depending on which level you are standing on when you view something. The following is a basic explanation intended to be viewed from the purely, physically human level of understanding. Unfortunately, as we have found when we explored other lessons together, the easiest way to look at something from a human perspective is not always the most accurate.

Because of this, without a doubt, this chapter and the following chapter should be used as an informational orientation point, of sorts. These chapters are meant to give you a touchstone which you can use to cut through the confusion that runs rampant throughout the purportedly spiritual information you are apt to run into in your earth life. There is much confusion and uncertainty among your peers about whom and what is going on.

Do not let anything you read within these two chapters cause you distress; for you will come to know, in the remainder of the lessons contained in these pages, what is truly important to focus on. And when you do, you will be able to see what is truly important and realize that there was nothing to worry about at all.

Recall, if you will child, that there are many levels of change going on around you. It is my intention with these lessons to help you forgo the noise of the lower frequency discord and move directly to the higher energy awareness where all truly should wish to be. To this end, it is best to keep in mind that greater divine spiritual work is not dependent on absorbing lesser imperfect concepts that stem from deeper in the illusion of physical reality. Also be mindful, because the information about to be presented in this and the next chapter is for orientation purposes aimed at those who live in a physical world, a large section of this and the next chapter are bound to sound very physically entrenched and not particularly spiritually motivated.

Do not fret over this. There is a great spiritual force to all that is about to be imparted to you, but for the sake of clarity in the form of a simple, down to earth explanation that can be followed from the dream, many of the more celestial aspects and higher revelations connected to the concepts in this and the next chapter have been purposely omitted in order to make it easier to follow for those in human form.

So, with this in mind, let us move on.

There are many players in the earth game. Some are easy for you to see, such as the human beings on the earth around you. Some you may know about, such as those beings that are commonly labeled angels, demons, spirits, and perhaps even extraterrestrials. There are others you may not be aware of who do not exactly fall into any of these categories.

One thing they all have in common is that they were drawn here to this earth node in this time and place in the dream, because they wish to be players in the segment of the grand game of Creation that is taking place on the earth.

As you know from our previous lessons, child, the balance of negative and positive energy in reality is always in exact balance. But until this point, there has always been a tilt in the balance in favor of positive energy in the dream that is the physical universe. This majority is slight, but it is enough to keep the darkness from overtaking all physical creation and destroying the learning cycle that keeps actual Creation itself alive. This margin of positive energies over negative is precarious at best, and fluctuates in and out of dominance at times for the briefest of moments. Nevertheless, it is, and must be maintained at an advantage overall.

Each node, in its own time, will come to a point where this energy balance will come into adjustment, or tuning. In the physical universe, this happens in a linear fashion, since time is constant in the physical universe, and moves in a linear fashion. So, over time, every planet which has a sentient life form on it will have its turn to adjust the balance of energy of itself, based on the tone and direction of the energy of the consensus of the beings living on it.

Some planets will naturally tune to negative influence without resistance. This is expected and must happen to keep the balance. Some planets will tune to positive influences naturally without resistance. The conscious life forms that live on these worlds are, by nature, created in the dream to be positive or negative to suit their worlds. Therefore, their home worlds will always reflect their own nature. In this regard, we can say that a negatively tuned world is, indeed, a *good* thing for its negatively focused inhabitants.

Such planets, regardless if they are positive or negative in nature, will remain the way they are because the beings who live on these planets have grown, at least until the point of their previous point of tuning, to their true planet's tone. They are creatures of their world, and their tone, energy, and frequency reflects perfectly with their world, be their home world's energy node positive or negative in its construction in the dream. Thus, if their planet was created to be a negative influence on the growth of creation, it tunes to support that goal. If their planet was created to be a positive influence, it tunes to support that goal.

There are those planets whose tunings are not assured. These are planets, like earth, that have been corrupted by other races before it came to its point of tuning. Because the human beings tone is not natural to the earth, for humans have been changed and corrupted over time by outside civilizations' physical interference, the human creature, as a source of motivation and direction for the tuning of the earth node, does not have any inkling as to what direction to take. There is an abundance of both positive and negative human mindsets of what should happen to the earth node, and many more mixed opinions.

Because of this confusion and indecision on the part of the human occupants of planet earth, it has effectively left the direction of earth's tuning up for grabs, so to speak. Earth could easily tune in either a positive or negative direction.

Over linear time, many races that have both positive and negative motivations have come to know about how planets tune and have come to understand how planets that have been corrupted no longer have a predetermined path. Such races consider these planets their's for the taking. They have also learned to read the signs and follow the pattern that shows which node is going to tune next and how to get to that node.

Since, linearly speaking, earth is the next planet in the succession of planets facing tunings, earth is the focus of many races and types of beings that all seek to manipulate the direction in which the earth's tuning will come to pass. In the most basic of terms, those who are primarily negative and want to see negative energy prevail, are here trying to invoke negative directions. Those who are primarily positive and want positive energy to prevail, are here trying to invoke a positive direction. Those who, like the Earthers themselves, are mixed in their motivations, are here for their own reasons, which for many — but not all — involves the gathering of power.

As I said, this is the most basic of explanations. There are many visiting here for other reasons as well. Those who fit in the categories above have many different motivations. We will explore who the major players in the earth game are and what they hope to gain from their endeavors in the next chapter. For now, let us look at the game itself.

Like any other game, the earth game has rules and referees. Also, like most games, the rules are sometimes broken by the players in order to try to gain an unfair advantage. When this happens, it is the job of the referees to step in and correct the matter. You may ask, child, who are the referees? Who maintains the rules?

The answer is a paradox of sorts. In short, there is no one who makes and enforces the rules. Rather, everyone involved in the game maintains the integrity of the rules, even if they break them. Confusing indeed.

There is a balance you could conceivably call justice to true reality, though the dream may be at times quite unfair. In reality, all things balance out. How can identical and completely complementary things not balance each other in all ways? Yet, in the dream, no one, not the most sainted of great masters, is truly and completely balanced to the ultimate divine. Nevertheless, child, the closer a soul is to reality, the closer that soul is to the justice force caused by this balance; thus, the less likely it is to do anything that would cause the soul to lose its balance.

Creation's justice is not a punishment force. It is a true understanding force that seeks out balance. Remember, child, everyone and everything with consciousness in Creation is exactly the same. It is only the focus and amount of your consciousness you have allowed into the dream that differs. It differs so totally from all others in the dream, that you, child, are unique. We are all unique and identical at the same time. What is truly wonderful is that each unique individual is not only identical to every other unique individual, but also identical to Creation — or if you will, God. The balance that is found in the pure Creation Force is actually in the total of each and every individual. So, as we can see, it is every individual's depth in the dream and distance from the awareness of his or her Oneness with the total of Creation that allows each to err by way of losing this balance. It is also this distance from the understanding of the total of the Creation Force that leads souls that lose sight of their balance to believe they must face the judgment of an angry deity.

With this in mind, child, it can be understood that when each consciousness ascends to the One Creation Force, that individual will understand that all he or she has done was to assist the growth of Creation, and no real rules were broken. For in the pureness of true reality, there is no need for rules. Rules are an illusion created to help give structure to the dream. The breaking of rules causes conflicting forces to collide and creates friction so that growth is possible. Rules are an invention of the dream, and are limited to the dream. They are enforced by those in the dream. In the case of the earth game, and other tunings like it, rules are enforced by the greater consciousness of those whom dare to break them.

The paradox contained within the fact that the earth game has rules and referees to enforce those rules, yet those rules are not truly enforced by anyone who can be named or pointed to as the enforcer , may be confusing to you, my child. Nonetheless, it is true, that is, within the limits of the dream in which it exists. There are consequences for breaking these rules that are exactly the same for everyone, yet, at the same time grow in severity in relation to the spiritual understanding of the being that transgresses. After all, the rules to the earth game are designed to bring some order and structure to the dream. The rules are as constant as other rules in the dream, such as the law of gravity. All seem constant, but in fact, all can be circumvented by those who know how.

With this in mind, let us explore the rules.

Rule one: Only those actually residing on earth as Earthers can produce the actions that make actual physical change with regard to the tuning.

This means that only beings in Earther bodies living on the planet are allowed to do physical things that will change the direction of the future in direct respect to the tuning. It is important to note, child, that the term Earther is not exclusive to human beings in this instance. Other sentient creatures natural to the planet are also included under this label, including but not limited to elephants, dolphins, and the great apes. Though, child, in this book of lessons, let us assume we are talking primarily about humans when employing the term Earther.

Rule one states that only physically incarnate Earthers can make the ultimate decision as to what the earth will be like after it is tuned.

This rule is intended to tie the hands of undue influence from outside sources. A non-earth life form, abiding by these rules, is restrained from coming to the earth and changing anything using their own influence by way of corporeal actions.

Unfortunately, this rule is often broken. Usually, the closer to the physical state, and thus, the lower the vibraton of the race or being, the more likely that race or being will physically interfere with the Earther's condition and situation.

There are exceptions to this rule. Beings of certain physical levels are allowed to interact with Earthers on a physical level that could change the outcome of the tuning.

This is limited to those whose own physical existence is close to the Earther's limited type of physical existence in the dream. Beings you may label extraterrestrials, although not all are strictly from outside the Earth's realms, fall into this category. This type of intervention is allowed for several reasons.

The first is that the people from other physical planets or other physical earth realms come from an environment that, like that of the earth, is not pure to its own tone. Thus, they are not purely positive or negative in intent and are not driven to one extreme or the other. You may rely on this fact, child. If any race of physically based beings is here on earth, regardless of what they may claim about their intentions and motivations, they themselves come from a planet that is also an unsettled node in the universal mesh. We know this because beings who are totally comfortable with the frequency of their planet, and in complete harmony with their world, are not inspired to leave it. Indeed, the thought of leaving such a perfect home and perfect frequency and tone would be unbearable to them. Therefore, they would have no need or want to invent the type of travel technology required to leave their perfect home and come to the earth.

Please understand, child, the above does not necessarily apply to spirit beings that come from other worlds that have tuned to a nonphysical frequency. For once a planet has tuned to a nonphysical frequency, the beings that live there can see past the limits of time and space, and can be anywhere, anytime, and still be home where the frequency suits them best.

The second reason why physical interlopers are allowed to interfere with Earthers is that such beings do not gain sustenance on the energy emitted by positive or negative emotions, and they have no interest in fostering false emotions in those they contact. Though it must be noted that there are many types of nonphysical based beings who do gain there sustenance on the emotional energy of Earthers, and often these beings will disguise themselves as extraterrestrial visitors, if only to add confusion to the game. Do not let yourself be fooled.

Another reason why their intervention is allowed is that it was their intervention that caused the frequency to go astray in the first place. Their current interference here is not going to add to the discord.

The last reason is arguably the most interesting. When every one of these different physically based races, extraterrestrial or extra-dimensional, first contacted the Earthers, they were without knowledge of the tuning, so their original intent was not to affect the outcome of the tuning in any direction. It is true, many of these life forms learned this information later. Yet, since their first contact was not one whose intent was to influence the tuning of this world, it did not break any rules. And since their knowledge of the tuning came after their arrival, they have the right, at least as far as the rules go, to stay. That is not to say that they cannot be forced to leave if they extend their influence too far into the affairs of Earthers in a nonproductive way. And, indeed, my child, this has happened more than once. It is wrong to say the motivations of these interlopers could not, or indeed, have not changed over time. In fact, without a doubt, it is more accurate to say that the more each race of extraterrestrials learns about the tuning, the more it tries to get its hands into the proverbial pie.

Though much text and time has been given to the races of nonhuman residents of planet earth, such as those described as Grays, Nordics, and other types of extraterrestrials, their involvement in the greater picture is not as important as even they would like to think. The only reason why these races are perceived as key players in the earth game is because the human consensus has created that role for them. It is interesting to note, child, that if the earthly media did not help to create an illusion of the great power and influence such races have, and then give that influence a sinister motivation, the role of such beings would be very different today. It is fortunate that the beings who share the Earther's physical proximity are few in number when compared to those with no physical presence, such as spirits. It is less likely extraterrestrial interloping will taint the tuning.

The farther away from the physical dream and closer to reality a being is, the more respect it must give to this first rule. The penalties for breaking this rule are as harsh on beings that human's consider immortals of divine nature as they are for beings that can be considered immortals of malicious nature. That punishment is simply the awareness that the rule was broken. It is the same penalty for all, yet it is far more impacting a toll to be paid for beings closer to perfection. Generally, beings of this description do not break this rule.

The only other exception to this first rule is when an Earther invests an abundance of personal energy into asking for intervention. In these cases, if the Earther cannot or does not know how to manifest his wish himself, intervention is sometimes allowed.

Rule Two: Suggestion is allowed; direction is not.

Any being of any affiliation, regardless of their status in the dream, may choose to suggest to any Earther an action, idea, or course, for any reason, even if that reason could affect the tuning. The being can transmit a concept, dream, impression, idea, or other information to any Earther to suggest a course of action, a state of being, or even a frame of mind. Yet, except for in rare cases, all are forbidden to give any Earther a direct order or command to do anything. To do so, would be to break the first rule.

Of course, as you might imagine, child, there are many ways around this rule. The easiest is to present a suggestion to an Earther in a deceiving way that makes the person perceive the suggestion as a direct order. For example, a being might imply that a person would find great joy by following the suggestion, or that a person would be in great pain if he or she does not follow the suggestion to the letter.

Rule Three: Earthers' energy given in prayer must be returned to them.

Every time an Earther prays, regardless of whom he prays to, the energy generated leaves the Earther and goes into other dimensions. Since many Earthers pray to a human-like, bearded, male deity who does not truly exist, the energy put into prayers is projected at the greater universal energies.

If a prayer is positive, the positive environment the person creates with his prayer makes it possible for positively influenced beings to enter into his life and help make the prayer come to fruition. More often, the positive energy of the prayer is absorbed by the positive balance of Creation, where it grows, and in time, returns to the Earther, allowing him to rewrite his own personal reality, even if he is not aware of what he is doing.

Much of the time, the power of prayer is positive in nature and has positive potential, but this is not always the case. Let us say that a man prays that God strikes his enemy dead, or a woman prays that God allows her rival to be humiliated in front of others. These are simple examples of when the energy given to prayer is negative in nature. When energy of this nature is sent to Creation in the form of prayer, the same things can happen to it, and more.

Like the energy of positive prayer, it can be absorbed by Creation, magnified, and returned in a stronger form to the one whom prayed, creating a negative environment around him. It can also inspire a being of dark intent to act on the request, much in the same way positive energies can inspire a being of light intent to intercede on the behalf of the one whom prayed. Both of these options are well within the rules, and do not violate the third rule in any way.

Rule three is most often broken by a class of beings many Earthers commonly call demons. These are beings of negative intent from a nonphysical existence and have no bodies, but are still deep in the dream in the realms around the very earth itself. These entities break the third rule by intercepting the energy given off in prayer — exclusively, negatively motivated prayer — and consume the energy as sustenance. By doing so, they do not allow the return of the energy to the person whom expended it in the first place. This is the violation.

Rule four: All beings agree that if they choose to enter the physical illusion as an Earther in order to have the ability to circumvent rule one, they willingly forsake any advantage, and come into the earth game at the same starting point all humans do, regardless of their original state of being and point of origin. Once these beings are physically embedded in the illusion, they are free to strive to regain what they left behind if they choose to.

This rule is the least often broken of all the rules that govern the earth game. This is because the physical bodies that are required to be a human cannot, by their nature, sustain many types of high frequency soul essences or consciousness. Or, in other words, there are few beings whose natural soul frequency is such that they would be able to be housed in a human body without doing such harm to that body so as to make physical life uncomfortable, if not impossible. Though many have tried. Indeed, child, if you suffer chronic illnesses, it is certainly due to this type of frequency discord between your body and your soul, and a frequency adjustment is in order.

As you know, child, earth is not the first world to tune. In fact, this is not the first time the earth has tuned. Everywhere in the physical universe where worlds have offered questionable outcomes to their tuning, this game has been played out. And it will be played out endless times more in an endless celestial sea of other worlds. Some of these worlds have other types of life forms that have physical bodies better suited to higher, more acute vibrational frequencies, and can house many more different types of beings than Earthers' bodies can. In such an environment, this rule is more likely to be broken.

Though it is not spelled out in this rule, some argue that the work certain extraterrestrials are allowed to do to the human body to make it a better receptacle and tool for higher soul frequencies to use, is a violation of this rule. This complaint is unfounded. These alien beings are, in fact, in the illusion at much the same physical level as the humans they interact with. This allows them greater latitude with regard to rule one.

Rule five: Any being with the ability is free to occupy the physical body of any other being whose body has the ability to house it, so long as both parties are agreed. No such exchanges should take place if one party is against the process. The owner of the flesh will always retain ownership of the flesh if they wish it.

This rule governs interactions between species, spirits, and beings that take place in a physical to nonphysical exchange event. Primarily, these types of events are called channeling, hosting, and walking in when the exchange is done with a positive energy being; and demon possession, cursed with devils, and under satanic influence when the exchange is done with a negative energy being.

This category has its own set of sub-rules that govern how these interactions are to take place. The most important of all the rules is that the exchange must be of mutual consent.

Who would willingly consent to being possessed by demons, you may find yourself wondering when you read this. The answer, child, may surprise you. Many people unwittingly ask to be possessed by demonic forces. Demon possession can occur if a person willingly asks for help from "God or Spirit" to do something evil. For example, if a man prays to God to give him strength to kill his enemy, he is inviting demon possession. Possession by demonic forces is not always like you have come to see on the television and in movies. It can be very different in appearance and manifestation, but the result is always the same. The person in physical form will always suffer due to the interaction, though this might not happen in obvious terms. Often, the physical host is used by the demonic force to hurt others before the demon does any harm to its host. It may even feed the host with a sense of power and excitement to keep the host in agreement, so it can continue to do its work.

By and large, the following rules are followed by beings of positive intention. Surprisingly, most beings of negative intentions do not have to break these rules to get what they want. They can circumvent these rules easily, because the majority of humans who engage in channeling related activities are not educated in the dangers they could encounter. Many will move blindly forward without regard, or even forethought, as to the nature of their spirit contact, thus, ask for any contact without proper limits that would invoke the rules. In short, the passion and desire to channel is so great that the person is willing to channel anything at all. This leaves the door open to anything, including unkind things, to take advantage without breaking any rules. Nevertheless, there are rules and sub-rules as to the use of another being's body.

For your reference, the sub-rules that govern the use of another being's physical body are as follows:

   a) No spirit-based life form shall willingly abuse a physical body for the sake of the physical experience.

Beings who have not experienced physical existence in the dream, or have not experienced it for a long time, may long to have the physical experience. These beings may want for physical sensation so much that they would be willing to experience the extremes of pleasure and pain in order to get as much a taste of physical life as they can have in the short time they are allowed to have hold of a physical body.

It is the responsibility of all beings who enter another's flesh to control their actions and do nothing inappropriate.

This rule is generally adhered to by positively focused beings, but seldom followed by the opposing side.

With the exception of those rare individuals who are called "walk ins", no spirit being is allowed to occupy the host body for more than the required time it takes to do the particular job
.

   b) The occupation of a host body by another being is not limited to humans. Beings are within the rules to occupy the bodies of other creatures of the earth, so long as it is in their ability to do so, and the transfer is consensual.

c) Occupying entities are not limited to beings who have no bodies. Any beings with the ability are within the rules to make a mutual exchange with any beings in physical form, even if the occupying beings have a physical body of their own.

d) Occupying beings who have physical form are not bound by rules that govern non-corporeal beings that enter a host's body. By virtue of their own physical placement in the dream, they cannot be bound by the rules beyond it.

In total, these five rules govern the way the earth game is played. They control, at least in theory, the forces that surround the earth, to different degrees and in different respects. There are those who follow them closely, and those who do not. When the rules are broken, there is the universal justice force of consciousness that resides in each being that keeps the transgressions in balance. The further a class of beings is from the source of Creation, and the closer they are to being a part of the physical illusion aspect of the dream, the more likely it is for them to break the rules. Also, the more likely it is for them to break the rules and not face immediate reprisal. Because of this, beings who are part of the earth illusion are more likely to believe they have gotten away with their transgressions and continue to perpetrate the wrongs they are committing. Though they will understand their errors eventually, the corruption they cause is often quite damaging to the other physical beings on the earth they have interacted with.

Though I must remind you, as we explored in a previous lesson, in true reality there are no mistakes made. What you would call transgressions and wrongs in the illusion where you are, are exactly as they should be in Creation. A paradoxical thought indeed, for in reality, no transgressions or wrongs truly ever happen. That is in reality, but for now we are speaking of the dream, and the rules that govern those who play the earth game.

Of course, human beings are not subject to these rules. It is the non-Earthers who are in human form who are subject to these rules. If you are reading this, it is extremely likely you are among these. Yet, your depth of involvement in the earth illusion may insulate you from these rules.

Now you know the rules. Let us explore the players.

Lesson 3

The Players

As we look at who is playing the earth game, child, we have to keep several things in mind. There are more than just positive and negative forces involved. There are more than just good guys and bad guys. There are many different types of beings involved for many reasons. For the sake of example, child, people tend to classify them into three major categories:

The good — those whose focus is to tune the earth in a positive direction.

The bad — those whose focus is to tune the earth in a negative direction.

The self-concerned — those whose focus is not the tuning of the earth, but of what they can get from the chaos the current confusion is causing, or what they believe they will get if their interests are defended and maintained through the tuning.

We will discuss several different types of beings in this lesson, but the discussion of spirits and humans will be left until the lesson found in chapter 4.

Currently, there are many different types of beings living on this earth that are not commonly known, especially when you include those who live in the spirit realms that surround the earth. Man is far from alone. Even before extraterrestrial beings came to this planet, man was not alone. There are many different types of beings who are also natural to this planet, though they occupy different dimensions which overlap or connect to the one that humans occupy. Many of these beings are, like you child, growing and learning about the times ahead. They are struggling in their own way to become a part of this mission earth, and are hoping for a positive tuning. Some of these beings are known to your people, although in recent years, many have questioned their existence.

Edge Beings

Life forms such as those you may label gnomes, elves, and fairies are all real beings. This may surprise you, child. Yet, I assure you, it is true. Although I must admit, the stories you may have heard about these beings and their ways of life are probably fanciful at best. Such beings as these, and many more, reside in dual dimensions connected to the plane in which you live. You could say that they live on the same earth as you do, but your vibrational location and there own do not exist at the same frequency. Thus, you quite literally live one on top of the other without any conscious overlapping of your separate illusion-based worlds.

On occasion, and under the correct conditions, such beings can pass through doorways, called edges, into this and other physical dimensions that are part of the earth's overall body. In recent years, because of deforestation and pollution in this layer of the earth, the number of valid edges has dwindled to near to none, and these beings are less likely to come across to this world, particularly in urban areas. Nevertheless, because their dimensional location is directly related to the earth's, their survival, and that of the earth, are intertwined to the point of no separation. If earth tunes negatively, their own existences will be negatively tuned as well.

Because of this fact, these beings are doing their best to become more involved in the world of the humans. As time passes, you are likely to hear more reports of these beings. If you live in a rural area, you are more likely to see them yourself. This is because they are realizing the peril their own worlds are in, and are making efforts to become players for the positive side in the earth game.

Earth-based Energy Eaters

In the category of energy eaters are the classes of beings who are native to the Earth and get their sustenance from the energies given off when humans experience emotional extremes. Although there are other beings that also gain nourishment from the absorption of energy generated by humans, those listed here have no other motives, aside from their own existence.

Shadow People

This ancient class of beings is sometimes labeled shadow beings or shadow people because they are often perceived by the sensitive as a shadow of a human outline that is much easier to see in one's peripheral sight. These beings have been with mankind since mankind has existed. They are a natural predator that came into being when the original earth tone was corrupted, just as germs did, and for the same reason. These things, germs and shadow people, were created as natural predators to destroy the invading tone. Please refer to our previous book of lessons for more information on the earth's reactions to invading tones.

Shadow people feed off the negative vibration of the human aura. They find their nourishment in the frequency a person gives off when he or she is in spiritual pain, emotionally disturbed, or involved in deception. Once they have established a feeding position with a human, they will encourage and create situations to perpetuate the pain and suffering in their human source in order to maintain the supply of food. Acting much like a long, terminal illness, shadow beings will feed on their victim slowly until the interference causes the death of their victim. They kill by means of disruption of positive frequency, which in time creates extreme frequency sickness. The frequency sickness becomes so intense that the victim will succumb to it and will die by way of a symptomatic physical or mental illness.

If there is enough food to go around — that is, if a person or group of people are producing sufficient negative emotions, these beings have been known to swarm in great numbers, much like sharks at a kill sight.

You may not always see shadow people lurking around their victims, but you can know where to expect to find them. They are the companions of liars. They thrive in times of war. Racism is like a sauce for their meat or cream on their cake.

Yet, regardless of how unpleasant they are, shadow people are not what could truly be considered evil. Though they do harm in order to sustain their food supply, they are only doing what comes natural for them to survive. They do not feed indiscriminately. They will never try to feed on a being that is not offering them the foul frequency they require for sustenance. True evil does not discern.

Yes, child, shadow people are beings that make a living by creating suffering, deception, and pain in humans. But you must understand, they are no more truly evil than a virus or a flu germ. They are dangerous and sometimes deadly; and care should be taken to avoid contact with them, as you would with a flu germ. But, child, they are no more to blame for their actions than the flu germ is.

If you have the ability to see them, and you see them around another human being, use caution approaching that person if you must deal with him. The presence of shadow people indisputably indicates that the person is in a mentally disturbed or spiritually comprised state that is causing him to produce the foul frequency that attracts and keeps these beings close. If you see these beings in your own home, you must contemplate your current state of mind. The presence of shadow people means, without a doubt, you, or someone else in your home, is providing them food. That food is always in the form of soiled frequency. Look at how you are proceeding and conducting your life. Are you true to yourself and others? Are you in an emotionally compromised state? Cleaning yourself of these darkness issues will stop their food and they will be forced to forage elsewhere. In the following chapters, we will learn about frequency adjustment and how to rid yourself and your loved ones of such beings.

Shadow beings have been mislabeled as everything from aliens from outer space, to devils, to figments of the imagination. They do exist, they are not imagination, and they are not from another planet.

They are not even devils. They are more like energy illness germs.

Glowing people

In a similar vein to the shadow people who eat the energy generated by negative emotions, are the ones who sustain themselves on the energy given off by positive emotions. These beings are sometimes mislabeled guardian angels, but they are not. When these beings are seen by sensitive individuals, they appear as glowing human forms just inside the peripheral vision. They are different from light beings that appear like balls of light, flashes of light, or bright white bodies. Glowing people always have a vaguely human body shape with no details, and they glow a faint, pale yellow or orange color. Like their shadow people cousins, they are attracted by energy given off by a person in a particular emotional state. In this case it is the feeling of calm, peace of mind, and the sense of euphoria.

Like their dark feeding counterparts, they were created when the earth tone was compromised as a germ-like entity. Unlike their dark feeding shadow counterparts, the purpose of these beings seems to be positive in nature. They infect the soul of the person they feed on and promote frequency's that are more in line with the original earth tone in order to create a steady supply of food. Even though their effect is pleasant, and the relationship they have with the human whom creates their food may seem more symbiotic than parasitic in nature, those who are in contact with such beings should always be aware that the emotional states created by these beings are not truly their own. Therefore, if the being moves on, the feelings will disappear with it, leaving the host feeling empty and low.

In general, these beings do not feed on any one person for very long, so little harm is done. That is, except in the case where these beings feed on the euphoria created by the false tonal frequency that accompanies some drug use. In such cases, the feeding only reinforces the artificial sense of reward, and can promote the addiction that both comes from and supports drug induced frequency sickness.

Child, you will discover that as the time of the tuning comes closer in a linear sense, many more people will gain the ability to see both types of energy eating beings. It may even seem to some that the world is suddenly being overrun with these entities. But you must remember that they have always been here, and in such numbers. It is simply that as the frequency of the earth rises, the frequency of those on the earth will have room to expand as well. Those working on expanding of self will begin to expand their own senses, and they will begin to see things that have always been there, just outside of their perception.

Child, do not let the energy eating beings upset you. Those that are glowing beings will not truly harm you, and those who are shadow beings will not care about you if you do not provide them food.

Elemental Beings

Unlike the elemental beings of some earth religions, the beings labeled herein as elemental beings are not limited to earth, wind, fire, and water. These beings are called elemental because they can be considered the basic energy/matter beings of the physical universe. Some are, in many cases, quite literally the intelligence behind the building blocks that make up physical existence. Others are universal forces that are constant across all of physicality. Here are examples of each type.

The Standing Ones

The Standing Ones are natural to your planet, and have been here on earth longer than mankind has. Indeed, child, they are natural to all planets and all physical matter in all of the material universe. They are the "ones who stand" that have been mentioned in ancient text. The Standing Ones are a paradox of sorts. They are bodiless beings in one sense, but in another, their bodies are so vast that they are impossible to truly comprehend, for their bodies are in the magnetic glue between every atom of physicality.

They are, for lack of a better way to help you understand, the glue that holds the physical universe together. They are a collective with one single mind, but they are made up of individual energies, each of its own frequency and tonal quality as needed to suit their work. They are called Standing Ones, for in energy terms, they would appear as strong, solid beams of force that create the transition of the pure energy of the spirit of Creation into the solid forms of the physical universe. They are mentioned in the ancient mythology of many peoples as the pillars that hold up the sky or the pillars of heaven.

Though they are separate from man and earth in a strict spiritual sense, they are present in every physical object in the pattern that holds the energy of that object's physical form. Therefore, what makes up their physical body is as vast as the physical universe itself. Thus, child, they are part of your physical body, too. Although, in all probability, you will never be aware of them.

The Standing Ones are unique in their position. They are alive and exist inside and outside the dream at the same time. They grow in number and change with the needs of Creation itself, yet they do not die or reproduce themselves in any way. They have no intelligence in any way humans can comprehend. At the same time, they are infinitely aware. They are also one of the few groups of beings who are truly neutral. They are not positive or negative in any degree. They do not care if a world or node tunes in a positive or negative direction. Their first and only responsibility is to the ultimate need of Creation.

In the case of earth, Creation requires it tune positively, thus the Standing Ones could be thought of as a strong ally on your side, so to speak. But I assure you, child, if it were in the best interest of Creation for the earth to have a negative tuning, and the Standing Ones did have direct interaction with people, the Standing Ones would work against you. They have no allegiance to positive or negative; to good or evil. They are not able to understand such primitive motivations. They are pure servants to Creation's will to maintain the dream. In truth, they are the essence of the magnetic force that holds the dream of Creation in the illusion.

Weather Spirits

Child, you may already be aware that there is an energy to the wind, rain, storms, and other weather events. You may have even experienced this energy when you had a breeze of wind blow in your face or warm rain run over your shoulders. Almost all people, even those without spiritual direction to their life, sense the energy in such things, even if they do not know the proper words to describe what they experience. But, child, did you know that there is an actual spiritual awareness to weather events. It may not fit into the toolboxes of all, but it is true. Weather events are based in elemental spirits. These are not spirits who, in general, can hold a conversation with you. For like all elemental spirits, they do not understand something as primitive as language. And, like the Standing Ones, they are truly neutral in nature. A warm summer breeze is no different in intent than a raging storm. They are just doing what they should.

There is an unusual aspect to weather elementals. Weather elementals exist all over the total of physical creation at the same time. The spirit of the wind in Maine is the same spirit in California, China, Jupiter, and a planet millions of light years away.

Another unusual aspect is that many things can influence weather elementals in local terms. People with the proper frequency knowledge can affect the weather patterns near to them without changing the nature or natural frequency of the weather elemental. It is true, child, that mankind can create copies of these elementals, and these copies may behave like the real thing, but do not have the same energy.

You, child, have experienced this yourself, I am sure. Take a moment to reflect how a cool, natural breeze is always more soothing and wonderful for your soul than the breeze from an electric fan. Ponder for a moment why a warm summer rain on your skin feels better than any shower you have taken. Though the air being moved by the fan is real, and the water from your shower is real, the natural energy that is delivering these things to you is missing, and thus, artificial wind and rain lacks that "certain something" you can easily feel. It lacks the energy of the elemental spirit.

There are many more elemental spirits that function much the same as those mentioned above. Rather than listing them all, let us move on, dear child, to other players in the earth game.

Animal Souls

Although it can be argued that most of the animals and plants living on the earth are not concerned with the greater earth game, it is clear that the outcome of the game will have a great influence on them, so it is for this reason I list them here.

All animals native to the earth have a structure of soul which has three separate layers. The greatest of which incorporates all animals into one being. Certain animals, such as most sea mammals, elephants, great apes, and mankind are not a direct part of the animal soul structure.

The first layer is in the animal itself. Philosophers and theologians have argued that animals are not self-aware and have no concept of their own state of life or death, thus proving they have no souls. This is not true. Anyone who has had a beloved pet knows that even the simplest of animals shows signs of knowing the stages of their existence and their impending death when the time comes. The first layer of an animal's soul is this layer. Its intelligence, its instincts, and its emotions as an individual creature make up this first level of soul.

The second level of an animal's soul is the greater group soul. All dogs belong to a greater dog energy that they return to when they die. All horses return to their greater horse soul, all kangaroos return to the greater kangaroo soul, and so on. After the animal returns, it is born again into another body of the same type of animal. A horse will always be a horse. It will not come back in the body of a cat. Likewise, once a mouse, always a mouse.

The indigenous peoples of North America were aware of this. They honored the greater soul of the animals they lived with and hunted for meat, because they knew that the consciousness of each kill they made returned to the greater soul and would eventually be born again. These people connected with the higher animal soul and shared with it. To be one with the eagle was not to be a kin to a single bird, but rather to be united with the greater spirit of all eagles.

The third level is one all earth animals and plants share, even those mentioned that do not take part in the first two levels. That is, with the exception of man. This third level is that of the greater total of life on earth in union with the earth. All animals — with the exception of man, for man is so out of tune he can no longer connect — join together on an upper level of energy that is shared among all things natural to the earth. This energy includes the animals, bugs, fish, and plants. If the original human tone were not so compromised, man would also become a part of this divine union with the spirit of the Mother Earth and all her creatures.

Elephants, Water Mammals, and the Great Apes

Elephants, most water mammals, and the great apes are exceptions to the typical animal soul stucture. This is because these creatures have a higher awareness that can be, if the individual animal wishes, focused on spiritual issues. An elephant can ponder the depths of eternity and find answers there to the questions it asks itself. A dolphin can reach out in prayer to be one with the Creator and feel enraptured in that unity. A mountain gorilla can struggle with its higher self over the meaning of life.

The ability to see past the issues of self-comfort, survival, and basic moral rights and wrongs is beyond that of most creatures mankind puts in the classification of the animal kingdom. Yet, if mankind classified animals by the types of souls they possess, he would find that he has more in common with an elephant than he does with his favorite house cat.

Like mankind, elephants, great apes, most water mammals, as well as a few other creatures on earth have a level of consciousness that is more than that of a simple animal soul. These gifted creatures, man included, have the ability to make deliberate choices using complex moral and spiritual understanding to do what is good or what is not.

This means, child, when a tiger, bear, or other animal with an animal's soul becomes angry, lashes out and kills, it has only done what came naturally at the moment, and is not morally responsible for its actions. When an elephant, orca, or orangutan does likewise, it has committed murder.

Plant souls

This leads me to the explanation of plant souls. You may ask yourself, child, could plants have souls in the same way humans or animals do? The answer is twofold. Plants do not have souls that are the same as humans or animals, but they do have souls in their own way. Plants and trees have different types of souls as well.

Each plant or tree has a life force and energy. That life force resides in the plant or tree and can be affected by some things around it. When the plant or tree dies, some of that life force is transmitted to the animal that consumes it, in the case of something being eaten; and to the ground, where the remainder of its body rots back into the soil, in the case of plants unconsumed.

When an animal's body rots back into the soil, the soil is enriched by the breakdown of the physical matter and the energy held in that matter, but the soul energy of the animal is separate from the body, so no soul energy goes into the soil. Plants and trees, on the other hand, have their soul energy affixed into their physical form, thus, part of the soul of the plant or tree will go with its flesh. The other part of the soul of the plant or tree returns to the energy of the greater plant self. For example, child, it may be hard to conceive, but it is true nevertheless, that there is a greater soul for each plant and tree that lives on the earth.

The greater plant souls, by their nature, have an energy that humankind can tap into if they wish. This is why certain plants can ward off illness or bring health just by their very presence in your body. It is not the plant itself, per say, but rather the energy frequency absorbed from that plant. Sometimes these frequencies manifest as chemicals that can be scientifically measured.

Trees are like plants with one exception. Tree souls also act like antenna, or lightning rods of sorts, to help the soul of the Mother Earth collect energy from the greater cosmos. When a tree is cut down, there is that much less connection between the being known as Earth and the universal energy source where she draws her sustenance.

Extraterrestrials and Extra-dimensionals

Some of you, child, will, during the course of your mission, come across beings who come from other planets or even from the unseen dimensions that intersect with that of planet earth. In general, beings from other dimensions that intersect the earth's, as with those from the realms around the earth, will be of a predominately positive nature and will be working for a positive tuning of the earth. This, as mentioned before, is because such beings have a sincere stake in the result of the earth's tuning, as they exist in places connected to the earth, albeit places unseen by humans. If you are lucky enough to ever encounter a being from another dimension or realm, you will find the experience eye opening, and perhaps even life changing.

When we turn our attention to beings from planets beyond the earth, we find that more discretion is required, as just about every different type of alien has a different agenda. Unlike spirit agendas, many extraterrestrial agendas are not basically positive or negative in nature. Often, the extraterrestrial agenda is so convoluted they themselves may be unsure what they are truly here to do.

Indeed, child, the convolution of good and malicious intentions is not limited to the extraterrestrial agenda. It also extends to the alien beings themselves. There are no alien races in physical form on planet earth who are without their own personal agenda. There is no alien race, council, or collective that you will ever encounter that is free from self-serving motives. This is a fact that is easily proven. Any being, race, council, or group of beings who have physical bodies in the illusion, even if they do not use those physical bodies to contact you directly, are so immersed in the illusion that it is impossible for any of them to be totally free from the pitfalls intrinsic to physical existence. And the greatest pitfall, of course, is the need to fulfill self-interest. Even if the words and the actions of alien beings seem altruistic, rest assured there is something they are getting or expect to get from the deal.

Consider this, would races existing deep within the illusion of physical reality and bound by the limits of the illusion, willingly expend the time, effort, natural resources, and expense it takes to manufacture spaceships, train crews, and send them to the earth at such an uncertain time in the earth's evolutionary life and expect nothing in return? Certainly not. An individual extraterrestrial may be so magnanimous with its time and resources, assuming any individual could have such resources, but an entire frequency sick population of a world with a corrupted tone of its own to sort out would never be so magnanimous if there was no payback expected.

How do we know the extraterrestrials here on earth come from worlds with corrupted tones? As we spoke about in a lesson just past, if any beings lived on a properly tuned planet, and they themselves were without frequency discord, they would be so content they would never wish to leave their world. The perfection of their harmonic tone would be their contribution to the growth of Creation and they would not be driven to build spaceships to save the earth. Certainly, any who say they have done just that should not be completely trusted, because one lie often leads to another.

The only exception to this rule is when the extraterrestrials have evolved to a completely nonphysical state of being through the process of tunings. When a race of beings as a whole, and the entire node they live on, tunes so completely that it is one step from returning to reality and is no longer physically present in the illusion, the energy of some of the beings who lived on that planet may feel their experience would be helpful in other places where tunings are taking place. Thus, they may choose to return to the illusion as part of a "tuning team", so to speak. If they do, they may choose to use their previous extraterrestrial nature as a point of reference. Such a point of reference was used in our first book of lessons.

It is interesting to note, child, that many of you have extraterrestrial elements in your bodies. This does not mean that all of you, child, have been visited by aliens; although it is sure some of you have. It was alien elements in the natural Earther's DNA that corrupted the frequency of the earth and caused frequency sickness of this node in the first place. Some extraterrestrial visitors became aware of their mistake when the human DNA corrupted their own. And now they are working with the forces that wish to tune this planet with the hope they can sort out the DNA confusion they caused and correct the problems on their own planet.

There are other extraterrestrial visitors who have come in more recent times who tend to complicate the tuning efforts, as they see no harm in genetically altering things of the earth. But, by and large, they are not truly as much of a problem as they might believe. For indeed, the will of Creation and the power of the Earth herself is what drives the tuning forward. Knowing this, it is easy to see that interference from a handful of uninvited, foreign guests can do little to stop it.

Angels and Beings of Positive Intent

It has been written, and in great detail, particularly in the medieval ages by the Christian church, that there is a hierarchy of angels and angelic beings who, more or less, work like a heavenly military force. In the context of this broad description, it is not far from the truth. Nevertheless, child, almost all that has been so painstakingly written by the Christians of old about the levels, names, physical descriptions, powers, and jobs of those labeled the angelic hierarchy is entirely wrong.

Almost everything written about the angelic pantheon is as accurate and as factual as everything written about the Greek and Roman pantheons of old, or for that matter, as accurate and factual as the book Peter Rabbit is to the life of a real field rabbit. This realization will be hard for some to fit into their toolbox. If it is hard for you, do not worry. It is understandable that 1600 year old dogma is difficult to dislodge from one's paradigm, particularly when the dogma has recently found new life in many New Age religions. So, if it is hard for you to give up the idea of the many classes and ranks of angels, all having familiar names, golden hair, and feathery white wings, it is not a problem, as it will not truly affect your existence. For indeed, angels do exist. They simply do not exist in the way most people accept as true.

There are several different types of beings who could be labeled angels, depending on your perspective. Let us start with the type you are most likely to know about and should be able to fit into your toolbox. The first type of possible angel is what is commonly called a guardian angel. These angels are the higher-self, disembodied souls of individuals who were intimately connected to a person in the illusion, but they themselves have left the illusion. Their focus, as you may already know, is to be a guide and comfort to their loved ones left behind. Their motivations are pure and good; this is why they have gained the title angel. Yet, if a strict interpretation were to be applied to them, guardian angels would fall under the classification of spirits, or at times, ghosts. Since such angels are angels by choice or action, rather than by nature of Creation, guardian angels will seldom remain guardian angels for long. Once the people they are watching over pass out of physical life, they will move on with them.

Another form of being that is often labeled an angel, is that type of spirit who assigns itself to a person to help that person through times of trouble. In general, these beings are attracted to the person they help at the request of prayer. They will stay with the person, helping the individual use the energy of prayer to fix a problem, if it can be fixed, or at the very least, to endure the pain of the problem until such a time as things are settled. When things are settled, the being moves on. This type of being is generally a spirit in nature and is using rule three to return energy given off in prayer by a physical being in order to fulfill the prayer.

Of course, child, when a spirit's mission is to do such things as answer prayer, comfort the sick, support the weak, and so on, then that spirit would, by the definition most hold in their hearts, truly be an angel. But, if you look at the strict biblical definition, the being would not qualify. By biblical definition, an angel is an attendant and messenger of God, not a comforting force for man. This is why such dogma does not make sense in reality.

In fact, there are many types of beings who choose to pursue as positive a path as they can. There are those spirits who strive to stop injustice. There are spirits who are mindful of man's mistakes and work to correct as many of those mistakes as they can. All these could be called angels. There are individual's, some embodied, some not, whose chosen path leads them forward to do good most of the time. These, too, could be called angels.

What, then, is a real angel? One thing the Bible did get correct is that an angel is a being who is the closest to God. What this really means is that an angel is a spirit who is only a few, or even one step removed from being absorbed into the Oneness of Creation.

Though so very close to universal Oneness that it is hard to separate them in human terms, this particular order of spirit beings still have a sense of individual focus and freewill. Paradoxically perhaps, is the fact that they are so close to the Oneness that they develop such a pure frequency and untainted focus of positive creative energy they are not actually capable of committing any action that would cause negative effects. These beings have the freewill and power to commit transgressions, but doing so is inconceivable to the root of their very nature that they cannot do it. These beings are the ones who wear the true label of angel. These are the beings who are the right hand, if you will, child, of Creation, working in the dream. Their vision, understanding, and goodness are the closest any spirit can hope to come to perfection without passing completely out of the dream and into that perfection.

Such angels do much of their work with other spirits, helping them ascend to the angelic level. They do, at times, work with and teach humans and others whom are more deeply embedded in the dream.

You may be interested to know, child, that it is difficult to live so close to the total of Creation and the limitlessness of reality, and still function in the dream. Angels often have to endure paradoxical choices when they are faced with reality changing decisions where the positive and correct thing to do is sure to cause distress to other beings, particularly those whose nature is in opposition to any positive direction. And, of course, they know that the negative is a required force. To have a higher level of consciousness not only brings with it clearer understanding, but also brings with it the clear connection between all energies. Angels understand, and indeed live the truth, that All is One. Thus, they feel the reactions to all their actions. Recalling the fifth principle of reality that states; everything in reality has a complement. This complement is totally and completely opposite in every way and detail to the original. Moreover, everything is identical to its complement in every way and detail. There is no difference between a piece of reality and its total opposite. Angels live true to this principle closer than any other positive beings. They feel all that happens to their complement when they take any action. They face the paradox that evil is a necessary good. It is only the angels' steadfast conviction to the success of the positive force of Creation, and their almost complete understanding of all of reality, that makes the balancing of their work possible.

Demons and Beings of Darkness

It is not in the best interest of our lessons to spend too much time pondering evil. Fortunately, the description of these types of beings can be easily explained with a few simple paragraphs. In fact, the information in those paragraphs would only be the exact opposite of that listed for beings mentioned above. Some darkly inspired beings may be spirits of people who have passed on, but have refused to let go of their anger or hatred of a person still living, so they follow that person from the spirit world, making as much trouble as they can. Other dark spirits are attracted by people who give off negative energy by way of negative prayer or focused rage. Sometimes, dark beings will wander around without clear direction looking for someone primed for their evil intervention.

Of course, if you follow the pattern, you can correctly assume that true demons are spirits from the closest levels to the ultimate Oneness of Creation.

They are as close to the reality of the Creator and as pure to their negative direction as angels are to their positive direction. You may find this fact hard to understand, child. But the reason is simple. As you know, outside the dream, in reality, there is no difference between a thing and its complement. Good and evil do not exist as they do in the dream. In true reality they are one in the same. The distinction only occurs when the energy moves into the dream.

Miscellaneous Beings

As stated before, child, the beings mentioned in this chapter make up a general list of the types of souls you are likely to encounter in your mission on earth. It does not mean that you are destined to meet all of these types, but some of you may indeed meet a representative or two from every group. There are countless other types of beings who you may come across on rare occasions, such as physically-animated/no-soul beings and non-intelligent energy patterns. Chances of you, child, encountering such beings are so very slim, it is hardly worth more of an explanation than to say that an eternal Creation has eternal options to give to the forms it chooses to bring into the dream. And indeed, we can logically assume this to be true, for we could never count and list them all.

Lesson 4
The Static and the Dynamic Soul

Author's note: It is important to understand, child, that in the next few chapters, when our lessons refer to frequency, unless otherwise stated, we are talking about the central frequency of the soul as it formed when it entered into the dream. This is different from the lesser frequencies each soul and body are subject to, or create from day to day.

Child, I am sure you know what humans are. That is, you know what a physical human is. You may even be one. More than likely, if you are even remotely interested in spiritual awakening and the tuning of the planet, you are a spirit in human form. Let us look at both types of humans — true humans and spirits in human form — and what each does for the earth and for Creation.

Let us start, shall we, with the question, what is a human? For if we start with the question of what is a spirit in human form, we indeed constrain our discussion to a rather limited subgroup of people on this planet. Only a fraction of a percent of the people living on the earth today are spirits in human form.

That is not to say, child, that few humans have souls. Indeed, every human, spirit in origin or not, has a soul. All souls are eternal. And every one is a perfect reflection of every one else in an eternal sense. This said, it must be pointed out that many people who walk on the planet today are here entirely for their own personal reasons that have the ultimate goal of just being part of the earth-experience. These reasons often include the experiencing of life and struggling to find purpose; which is attempted through a multitude of methods, not all of which accomplish the goal set upon. Along with such personal goals, true humans are strict disciples of the Mother Earth. They are working for her every day, at least in theory.

As you know, the earth has been afflicted with a type of planetary frequency sickness. This is the fundamental reason why she must experience a tuning. The humans who live on her are affected by frequency sickness as individuals and groups of individuals. Indeed, child, the frequency of the humans on planet earth is so fouled and confused that the majority of mankind are in such discord with the planet, rather than fulfilling their purpose of helping her, the things they do harm her greatly. Still, child, these true humans are part of the mechanism of earth, or in other words, the illusion of physical life on earth. Indeed, if these humans were not compromised by the invading tone, mankind would be a perfectly working cog in that illusion mechanism. Alas, it is not.

Aside from these humans who are a natural part of the earth illusion mechanism, there are other people who are physically human, but whose original state of being is not that of a human. What I mean by that, child, is that they did not leave Creation and enter the dream directly into the form of a human being with the purpose of being part of the earth. These beings entered the dream directly into a nonphysical form. When they entered the dream, they did not enter the depths of total emersion in the illusion of the physical on earth or anywhere else. And though many of these spirit beings did, over time, project some of their soul energy into the illusion in order to take on corporeal form on earth or other physical places, the origin of these beings remains nonphysical in nature. These are the beings that I refer to, child, when I use the term spirit in human form.

You see, there are two basic natural entry points into the dream for consciousnesses that wish to take part in it in such a way that they can affect its unfolding. The first is to come directly into physical form. The second is to enter directly into nonphysical form and later, if need be, take on physical form. Both of these ways have their advantages and drawbacks. Both are equally important to the growth of Creation.

The decision to enter the dream directly into physical form is based solely on the purpose of the part of Creation that is entering. A choice must be made. Is this part of Creation destined to be a static working part of a certain individual planet or place? Or, is this part of Creation destined to be a dynamic part of the dream overall? In the case of the consciousness that enters directly into physical form, the answer is that it is to be a static working part. For those parts entering directly into nonphysical form, the answer is that it is to be dynamic in nature.

Both soul types are identical reflections of the greater Creation Force. Both sing the universal song which consists of two parts, tone and frequency. In the case of the static soul type the tone is designed to be in harmonic agreement with the universal song and the frequency is designed to match that song exactly. In the case of the dynamic soul it is just the opposite.

The tone is designed to match exactly to the universal song and the frequency is designed to be in harmonic agreement.

This by no means implies that energy entering in one form is not as powerful or wonderful as energy entering in another form; for both are identical. It simply means that the function of the energy in the dream is different.

Let us start, child, by exploring what happens when consciousness enters the dream directly into physical or static form, as a static soul. When a part of Creation is called to the dream in physical form, it enters the dream directly to a node in the mesh of the physical universe where it will remain for as long as it is in the dream. The focus of this energy, upon taking on physical form, is to be an active part in the development of the particular node in the universal mesh where it took form, and only that node. The original form of the physical manifestation of the energy will be one in tonal harmony with the node. That is, child, if the node itself is of an uncorrupted frequency. In the majority of cases, this is how the nature of the physically embedded, static soul being will remain until it leaves the dream. It will be in harmony with, if not in exact frequency with, the tone of the place it originated, and will be a working and useful part of the evolution of that node as it moves towards the universal song. Since the soul is eternal, of course, child, the total of the soul is far too large to fit into one physical form. The vast majority of the static soul being remains outside the illusion in the greater reality around the planet of focus. In order to keep this link between two different densities of the dream, some of the energy of the original consciousness that entered the dream actually makes up the energy that holds the cellular structure of the corporeal representation in the illusion. This means that the body that houses the static soul is, at least to some extent, part of the soul on an energy level.

If I may move in a tangent to this lesson for a brief moment, dear child, this energy to body relationship in static consciousness is different from that in dynamic consciousness beings and thus frequency sickness and the healing of frequency discord must be approached differently for both types of beings. We will go into this in some detail in a future lesson. I mention it at this time because it is the root of many of the issues faced by embodied dynamic soul beings that seek out healing by methods created for the majority, who are, of course, static in nature.

Returning to the focus of this section, if I may be permitted; strictly speaking, human beings on the planet earth are, overwhelmingly, static soul beings. The Creation energy that makes up their souls and indeed, part of their physical presence in the illusion, came directly to the earth from the pure energy state. By the nature of their static form, these people are bound to the earth while in the dream. Their purpose for being in the dream is the progression of the earth node. Yes, they do have individual purposes to their existence, but their individual goals are inseparably intertwined with those of the earth. If the original earth tone was not corrupted, and if the natural frequency instructions for the creation of the human physical container were not also corrupted, all of the personal goals of the people on the earth would be for the greater good of the Mother Earth herself. But as we know, this is not the case. Many of the personal goals of static soul beings on earth are so off frequency that they are in direct diametric opposition with what they should be.

Static soul beings, regardless of their level of frequency discord, will remain with their place of origin until such time as they return to Creation. This does not necessarily mean the time of the being's physical death. For indeed, many static soul beings will only go as far as they need to outside the earth illusion to reset themselves to the universal order. This reuniting with the universal order is deep enough, in the case of static soul beings, to distance them from the lower frequency of their recent physical existence to such an extent that they will no longer be able to retain the low frequency. As a result, they will forget most, if not everything, about that previous existence when they once again return to their node of origin. This knowledge will be retained on a higher frequency level. Nevertheless, this distance is not far enough to truly and completely unite with the total Oneness of the pure creative consciousness where they began before they chose to enter the dream. So they remain static soul beings by nature and return to the node where they originally entered the dream.

In other words, by simply resetting to the universal order that can be experienced from the highest reaches of the dream, but not actually returning to be totally absorbed by the One true reality outside the dream's limits, these static soul beings are refocused and return to their point of static origin to begin again.

Many beings will take this course of action over and over until a node tunes. Others will give up their static existence after a few, or even one physical lifetime. When a static soul being physically dies and then physically returns by way of a new birth, it is what humans would call reincarnation. For the spirit of a static soul being is incarnate over and over again in the same basic form at the same place of origin.

Technically speaking, when a dynamic soul being enters physical form, it is not truly reincarnation. It is more accurately an embodiment or re-embodiment, as this spirit can take to almost any physical form in almost any physical node. If this were the only difference, child, perhaps you would accuse me of splitting hairs. It is not. What makes the true difference between the reincarnation of a static soul being and the re-embodiment of a dynamic soul being is the fact that dynamic soul beings are not subject to the total reseting of dream memory and can often embody themselves with recall of their total existence. On Earth, this is most often done for short periods of time, such as in channeling encounters. Certainly, dynamic soul beings are able to do this for full lifetimes, that is, unless they fall under the governance of rule four as stated in lesson 2.

Unlike static soul beings, dynamic soul beings enter the dream as nonphysical spirits. Their point of origin is nowhere and everywhere at the same time. Their tones are not focused on that of a particular node and are, in general, identical to that of the universal song. Dynamic soul beings are free to travel, if you will, from one node to another, taking part in events unfolding at any node they come to, if they wish to. Indeed, child, some dynamic soul beings were created by divine design to visit each node that is about to tune and assist with that tuning. In fact, as you know, like frequency will attract like frequency, so some dynamic soul beings have grouped together in what could be considered "positive tuning teams". These teams work together again and again, in a linear time sense, to bring about the tuning of various nodes in the universal mesh. You may even be a member of such a team.

Regardless of the direction the dynamic soul being is prone to take, if that being is required or requested to do work from the position of a physical body on a physical planetary node whose tuning direction is in question, the dynamic soul being is subjected to rule four and agrees to enter the dream under the same conditions as a static soul being would. In other words, he or she will be born into a physical body with little or no knowledge of any previous existence or condition.

Since the static soul beings on the earth are so confused by tonal discord and frequency sickness, it is impossible for these beings alone to choose the proper direction to which the earth needs to tune in order to fulfill the need of Creation. This is the same on just about all worlds where the planet's original frequency is damaged and the static life forms on the planet have lost the connection to the planetary song.

How does Creation rectify this problem, and thus, have these planets of confusion tuned and set right? This is where the work of dynamic soul beings come into play. Since disembodied dynamic soul beings are not entrenched in the root tone of any physical node, but instead are attuned to the overall universal tone, and embodied dynamic soul beings have none of their soul energy embedded in the planetary matter they reside in, dynamic soul beings are able to make the choices static soul beings cannot.

In other words, child, dynamic soul beings have a clearer vision of what Creation expects from the tuning of a node.

This is an interesting paradox. Consider this, dynamic soul beings have an unchanging tone that matches the universal tone. Because of this, they cannot create an exact frequency that completely corresponds with the universal frequency or they will be in agreement with both universal tone and frequency and will transcend the dream.

Consider that in order for any physical node to be harmonically tuned, the node's tone must be in parallel synchronization to the universal tone, but it must not match exactly; and the frequency of the node must be in total agreement with the universal frequency. Consequently, in order to bring a misaligned planet into tune, the frequency must be adjusted to match that of Creation, but the tone must be adjusted so that it does not match exactly. As you can see, child, this clearly shows that dynamic soul beings are not designed to tune any node. Yet, they are the only ones who can tune nodes. A paradox, indeed.

Whether they know it or not, static soul beings on any ill-tuned node are striving for an exact frequency match to the universal song, and they sense dynamic soul beings as a challenge to this match. This causes a conflict that can, and sometimes does, cause extreme difficulty for dynamic soul beings. This is especially true for those whom have entered into the physical state in order to help with a tuning, such as you, child. The very people you are helping the most will be those who resist you the hardest.

For the most part, static soul beings will simply ignore what they do not perceive as important to their own goals. This is why so few people around you, even those who appear to be concerned with the state of the world, are not interested in or have no wish to even hear the most simple of spiritual principals. These things plainly do not interest them. Some will even feel threatened by your way of thinking and may even argue against you. This is also an expected response. In some cases, if you allow yourself to fall into games of negative energy play, you may even find yourself facing outright attack of a verbal nature, or worse. Remember, child, this is only a danger if you allow yourself to go so low as to engage such a person on his or her own frequency level.

These things happen because there is a percentage of static soul beings, whom, by virtue of their frequency sickness, interpret the strong desire embedded in their soul to do what is correct for the earth-tone as hatred of anything they perceive to be different from themselves.

As we explored in a previous lesson in the first book, frequency sickness is more than just a condition that causes physical symptoms. It also binds those with similar foul frequencies together and incites them to fight to dominate any other frequencies. This binding of like frequency is the true root source of all wars on earth. There are so many masses of frequency sick populations on the earth with so many different frequency disruptions, that it is no wonder you are bound to find some people whose frequency sickness will lead them to be in opposition to your frequency, regardless of what your frequency is. The stronger and more focused on universal light your frequency is, the less likely you are to be harmed by these people and their desire.

In the same train of thought, child, because of the universal nature of the central tone and the flexible frequency patterns of dynamic soul beings, they can never be fully in tune with a physical node until after that node is in full harmony with the universal song the dynamic soul beings sing. This means that for as long as a dynamic soul being is working in corporeal form on a planet, the frequency of the dynamic soul being is subject to waves of physical symptoms if their frequency is not frequently adjusted to a harmonic tone with both the planet and the universal song.

You, child, may find the reason for this interesting. Unlike static soul beings who have a percentage of their energy essence embedded on a quantum level in the cellular structure of the physical body they inhabit, dynamic soul beings do not, and indeed, cannot make their energy part of the body on any level. As you may know, child, all physical things, including bodies, on any planet are made from the matter of that planet, and thus they belong to the energy of that planet, given that matter is merely energy in physical form. Since static soul beings are designed to be a part of only the one planet they originate on, it is natural that some of their energy goes into the physical cellular structure of the bodies created for them. By that I mean, the energy particles that are beyond microscopic, those on the quantum level, that create the basic relationship between the energy of the being and the matter of the body created for it in the illusion, are taken from the static soul being's total energy body. This intermixing serves to more solidly unite the energy of the static soul being and the energy of the location of its origin. Since dynamic soul beings are not created to be a part of any one planet, but are, in fact, created not to need to be part of any planet, the quantum material that connects their energy physically to the illusion when they choose to enter into corporeal form is not suited to any planet and will not, and indeed cannot, take on the form of that planet. Thus, the energy needed to form the quantum connection is taken from the planet, which naturally moves in to do the job. What this means, child, is that the physical bodies created for, and employed by, dynamic soul beings hold no part of the natural frequency of the dynamic soul being in their quantum coding.

This means little in the mode or use of the physical body by the spirit to interact in the physical world. But it does make a great difference in the types and symptoms of frequency sickness that can affect the dynamic soul being, as well as the means to heal such frequency sickness. In addition, it is also the key to a dynamic soul beings ability to bring a node into harmonic agreement.

Dynamic soul beings' central tone is tuned to the universal song before they enter a physical body. If the tone of the physical body is in harmonic agreement on a tuned world, all things will be good. When the central tone of the physical body a dynamic soul enters is in discord on a planet of corrupted tone the problem is twofold. Not only is the dynamic soul being now out of tune with the universal song, but the being is also out of tune with the planetary song. Because there are two distinct parts to the dynamic soul that are out of tune, there are two issues that must be put in harmony in order to cure frequency sickness.

This is not to say, child, that dynamic soul beings should have two frequencies to follow. Indeed this is not correct at all. As we have discussed in a previous lesson on the frequency of life in book one, every soul strives for and needs only one frequency in order to be complete. This remains true, regardless if the soul is dynamic or static in nature. However, where the static soul being requires only one source for that single tone, that being the planetary song of its own place of origin, the embodied dynamic soul being's single tone must come from a balancing of the purest tone to the universal song that can be maintained in harmonic combination with that purest frequency that can be found on the planet where they currently reside.

As I mentioned before, child, dynamic souls do not always enter into the dream in a corporeal form in order to help a node tune, though a few most certainly will. A vast number more will remain in spirit form and offer their assistance from the energy realms around the node. It is important to mention that only the dynamic soul beings that choose to take physical form can truly have physical influence over the tuning of the earth illusion. It is this select group of dynamic souls who have taken on the challenge of frequency discord in order to do the bulk of the tuning work. As a reward, they also receive the experience of physical life. Physical existence is not a natural form for dynamic souls. This explains why so many dynamic souls who embody themselves develop a stronger love of nature than most static soul beings on an ill-tuned planet. Unfortunately, it also accounts for the many dynamic soul beings that do not feel at home on any physical planet, and long to be somewhere else.

You may be asking yourself, child, why any being would choose to be a dynamic soul over a static soul or via versa. Indeed, the choice to come into the dream as a dynamic or static soul is made without any selfish considerations, from a spiritual level that is united in true reality, beyond the want of the dreamer. In other words, child, it is a perfect eternal reflection of a perfect eternal Creation that chooses when and how to move into the dream or the illusion. Or, if it will be easier to fit into your toolbox, it is the Creation Force, or God, who makes the choice to move an eternal part of itself into the dream as a dynamic soul, or deeper, into the illusion, as a static soul.

Although once in the dream, a soul's natural state will stay static or dynamic for as long as it is there, every soul is free to change their status when they return to the Creation Force beyond the dream. Once an energy enters the dream as a static or dynamic soul being, it does not mean it is destined to be a static or dynamic soul being for eternity. Once an individual energy focus gives up the dream and illusion, and returns to the Oneness of Creation, it is free to reenter the dream as anything it wishes, if it chooses to return at all. Of course, true unity with the Creative Force on a level beyond the dream will cause a total reunion with the universal song and the individual soul will no longer be an individual soul. It will be one and the same with the truth of reality. This holds true if the soul was static or dynamic in nature and regardless of any linear time restraints, which as you know, have no relevance beyond physical existence.

Thus, child, in summary, we can see that the difference between a dynamic soul and a static soul is the function each serves in the dream. The function is rooted in the point of origin of the soul, with static souls possessing a point of origin that makes them a part of physical planetary mechanisms, manifested in the form of sentient life; and dynamic souls possessing a nonphysical entry point in the form of spirits, who may or may not then take on physical form. Knowing the difference between these types of souls is important when addressing the detailed healing of frequencies that can cause cacophony in both types of souls when they take physical form on a node in need of tuning.

Lesson 5
The Nature of Repeating Expression

We have touched upon the concept of repeating expression many times in our past lessons, yet we have not spoken of it directly. We talked about it when we looked at the perfect reflection each piece of eternity is to the whole. We spoke about it when we talked of harmony of frequency. We even delved into it, ever so slightly, when we talked about the balance between positive and negative.

Repeating expression is a tool used to construct and maintain the dream. It is also used to layout the patterns of all things physical. Repeating expression is something you are very well aware of. You see it every day, yet in all probability, you give it little thought. Indeed, child, many who explore repeating expression are discouraged by others around them. Perhaps you have even been a victim of this yourself. Let us look at a simple, yet important example of repeating expression you have probably noticed in your life, perhaps as a science student. This basic example may have occurred to you when you first learned about the physical nature of the atom. Did you notice, child, when learning about atoms having a central nucleus that is encircled by spinning particles, how similar this structure is to that of the solar system? Many do make this analogy, and if they voice it aloud, inevitably someone will call them foolish for thinking it. Yet, child, as you may suspect, it is not foolish at all. It is one of the simplest examples of repeating expression.

There are both physical and mixed types of physical/nonphysical repeating expressions in the dream. There is only one repeating expression that is totally outside the dream. Our lesson for this chapter concerns those repeating expressions that mix the physical and nonphysical. Nevertheless, child, it would do no harm to talk briefly about those that are precisely physical in nature, and the one that exists outside the dream in true reality.

Physical repeating expressions are created by the natural vibrational frequency that extends beyond any one single node in the total physical dream in which they occur. For example, the repeating expression you will find in the physical universe where your planet resides will be a constant throughout all of that physical reality. Using the simple example of the atom and the solar system, we can see that galaxies also follow the pattern of having a single center and material that rotates around that center. Because of the grand physical size of galaxies, the amount of matter that spins around the center point can seem to be much more than that which spins around an atom or within your own solar system. But indeed, child, if you were to add in all the subatomic quantum particles to your vision of the atom, and all the smaller space objects, comets, and asteroids to your view of the solar system, I assure you the view would be as busy. If you had the ability to look at the total of the physical universe from an outside view, you would see that all things in the physical universe follow this pattern as well. Everything is seemingly flying away from a center point, in what earth scientists would call "red shift". If man's math assumptions and astronomical tools were good enough, and his life long enough to observe any substantial glimpse of actual galactic time, he would see that rather than a big bang, what he is observing is a big swirl.

Another physical repeating expression can be seen in the shape of life on earth. Consider that all life on earth, with the exception of insects, some fish, and some snakes, are tetrapods. All mammals, amphibians, birds, lizards, crocodilians, even dinosaurs for that matter, have four limbs. Many snakes and fish have indications of rudimentary limbs that can still be found in their anatomy. It does not matter if the four limbs are legs, arms, wings, or fins. Have you ever wondered since nature is, as we know, frugal in her design, why there are no three-legged life forms? Why has the earth never seen a species of bird with the two wings needed to fly, but only the one leg needed to perch? Why, since it is true that with only three legs you can make a strong and sturdy stand, did nature give most animals four legs, and some animals two legs and two arms or wings, but no animal at all was given three legs to walk with?

This is because life on earth follows a basic repeating expression that can be seen in the symmetrical characteristics of life on earth. Knowing that any repeating physical expression you find on earth is also inherent in the rest of the physical universe, it is no wonder that most extraterrestrial life forms are reported to be four limbed and bipedal.

Understanding the principals of repeating expressions, we can accurately assume that the majority of mammals, amphibians, birds, lizards, and crocodilians that may exist on any other planet, no matter how foreign an environment that planet presents when compared to what is found on earth, will have one thing in common. They will have four limbs.

Fascinating as it may be, let us move on, child, from physical repeating expression to that of the one and only repeating expression present in true reality outside of the dream, in the heart of the Creation Force. What is this one and only repeating expression? Some of you, I am sure, can venture to answer correctly. It is the truth that there is only one eternity, that it is broken up into an eternal number of parts that are, each one, eternal. Each one of these eternal parts is a perfect repeating expression of the original. Each piece of eternity is a perfect eternity onto itself.

Let us now move on and look at the types of repeating expressions that are pertinent to you and your mission here on earth. These, of course, child, are those repeating expressions that are both physical and nonphysical at the same time, what could be called mixed repeating expressions.

Mixed repeating expressions are wonderful and amazing things. They are the patterns that link the world of the spirits to the world of those in physical form. They are part of the pattern of your consciousness. They are also instruments to the soul in physical embodiment. If there were no mixed repeating expressions, there would be no way any energy being could become physically immersed in the illusion as a physical being with a conscious soul, in the sense mankind understands consciousness.

When examining mixed repeating expressions, one is often left looking at subatomic or quantum material that is not really physical but is not really pure energy in nature. It would be difficult, and in truth, it would be a waste of our time in this stage of our lessons to inquire into such hard to visualize examples. Luckily, there are a few examples that are easier to see from the current understanding level most of you, child, are comfortable with at this point.

So, let us take a look at two of these few examples of mixed repeating expressions, so you can get a general impression of what they are and how they work.

Without going into a long lesson about wavelengths at this time, let us agree, child, energy moves in waves. Waves of energy have, among other things, a frequency caused by vibration, and a wavelength or tone. The frequency is the number of repeating waves formed by vibration as calculated by how many times the pattern repeats itself in a particular time set. The vibration is, in simple terms, the energy that creates the frequency. Waveform is the size of the wave as measured from crest to bottom. Although there are many shapes waves can take, in order to keep this explanation simple, we will assume all our waveforms are smooth, simple sine forms. It is the size of the wave that creates the actual tone; it is the frequency that produces the pitch of the tone.

When you apply these things to the two types of souls, static and dynamic, you can observe two examples of mixed repeating expressions. Let us investigate the repeating expression in the static soul first.

As you know, both static and dynamic souls are identical in their eternal structure outside the dream, but will differ by the necessity of their function when they enter the dream. The static soul is the one that comes into the dream directly into the illusion of physical life in order to take part in the workings of a particular physical node in the universal mesh. As you are also aware, all energy is a vibrational frequency pattern. The tone is the original vibration that causes the frequency of a static soul to split from the One Creation Force. It is the pure universal tone. The vibration caused by this pure universal tone creates the original wave to form that is the tone of the static soul. Yet, by necessity, the static soul must fit into the unique tone already in the dream, that being the tone of the planet where it will find physical origin. That means that the original pure waveform must be adjusted so it can be brought into agreement with the planet's tone, and thus match the unique nodal tone that planet sings in the universal song. This tone should be in harmony with that of Creation, but not exactly the same. If it were exactly the same, the node would be indistinguishable from Creation and no longer exist in the dream. Therefore, in a harmonic scenario, the frequency of the wave that makes up the energy of the static soul will remain the same, but the tone will need to be adjusted down until it is occurring in the same harmonic interval as the planet the soul is designed to originate on. In other words, the number of waveforms will remain the same, but the size of these waves will change, cresting at a harmonic interval below the original tone. When the wavelengths synchronize in such a way, the node is considered in harmonic agreement with the song of the universe. This pattern of perfectly matched wave sizes is a repeating expression of a wave created by a vibrational frequency.

In the case of dynamic souls, since they are identical to static souls until they enter the dream, the energy that causes the vibrational source of the waveform is the same as that of the static soul, and thus, the size of the wave starts out the same. But since there is no need to diminish the tonal characteristic of the wave in order to bring it into harmony with a particular physical node, the original tone will not change. Yet, since there is no connection to a physical node, there is no need for a set frequency to bring out harmonic agreement with any particular node at this time. Therefore, since the frequencies of dynamic soul beings do not have to be fixed to a place, whatever natural frequency the vibration comes to rest at will be that which the dynamic soul will have to begin with. Thus, in the case of dynamic souls, the repeating expression is seen in the original wave height that remains the same, regardless of circumstances, but not in the frequency of the wave's occurrence, which can vary greatly from one dynamic soul to another, and thus one spirit to the next.

I understand some of you, child, may be confused, as I understand the words frequency, vibration, energy, and the like are often freely interchanged in the world around you. By frequency, in this book certainly, and in this chapter at the very least, I refer to what the word literally implies. That is, how often a wave pattern happens in a given time, and thus how frequent it is. When the waveform occurs more frequently, the frequency is higher. The pitch of the tone is also higher. When the waveform occurs less frequently, the frequency is lower. The pitch of the tone is also lower. This means a spirit of a high vibrational frequency is one whose natural energy state vibrates with more complete waves in a given interval, which causes a higher pitch than a spirit of a low vibrational frequency whose natural energy state has fewer complete waves. Since the wave is the tone that makes up the form of the energy given to the soul at the time it entered the dream, the wave is the true tone of Creation. It is the universal song. Naturally, a being of higher vibrational level, greater frequency, or if you will, child, a being whose natural energy has more exact copies of the true tone of Creation in it, would be a spirit of higher connection to the Creation Force — God.

In the case of an angel, the frequency is so high that the universal tone is repeated in their soul a virtually infinite number of times in a given interval. This near to infinite repeating expression of the original tone brings the angel as close as possible to true and full unity with the Creation Force by virtue of the infinite reality of the Creation Force. Notice, child, the repetition of the wave is near to infinite, but not infinite. If it were to repeat itself to the infinite mode, the angel would no longer have a presence in the dream, for it would be one with reality.

Understanding the true nature of exact frequency patterns is not a prerequisite for waking up your consciousness and living in control of the dream. You are not required to ponder such things. Though, if you do, you may find answers to the questions mankind has labored over since his earliest existence.

Nevertheless, I do not wish to stray too far from the topic of our lesson.

Returning, if I may, child, to the idea of repeating expressions, we can see that the frequency of the energy that makes up the dream is merely a repeating expression of the core tone of the universal song. This would be true if you were in a node where the natural frequency was not disrupted, the vibrational energy was not in discord, and the universal song was not so lost as to be only hinted to in the remnants of a harmony lost in the current cacaphony. In the worst of cases, it is not just the harmony to the tone that has changed the frequency, it is the harmonic tone itself that has been changed. This has happened to the people on the earth and to the earth itself. The original tone, that being the waveform the earth was created to resonate with in harmonic agreement to the universal tone, has not only been affected by frequency disruption in how often it occurs, but it has also been forced to change tonal shape. Keep in mind, that when the tone changed, it was at that point no longer in agreement to the tone at the root of the universal song. The repeating expression of the root waveform and tone of the universal song had been compromised, and thus, the node where this happened is no longer in tune with the rest of physical creation. When such a thing happens it creates a paradox in the order of the physical universe overall. But for now, I will leave that to your imagination and to a future lesson.

Since repeating expressions are interwoven with frequency and tone, they are important things for you to be aware of, even if they are a bit hard for you to fully understand. For indeed, child, all you truly are is a tone given to a form, and a frequency that form has settled into.

Before ending this lesson, I would like to revisit something important, if I may, child. That is, how the universal tone affects both static and dynamic souls when they enter physicality. As I have already mentioned, both static souls and dynamic souls leave the Creation Force under the vibrational energy of the single universal tone. Thus, both static and dynamic souls start out as perfect reflections of the universal tone. In order to become physical, static soul beings must be able to adjust the original tone to that of the world in which they enter. If that world is in tune, then this happens with the assumption that the world is in harmony to the tone. Thus, static soul beings are created with the ability to fluctuate their inner soul tuning to the universal tone to some degree in order to make a perfect match with their point of origin. In order to keep in harmonic agreement once they have adjusted to the new tone, static soul beings must maintain a constant frequency, so that the tonal waveform runs perfectly synchronized to the universal tone. Since frequency is an adjustable thing, it takes effort to maintain it in a place invaded with any discord.

Dynamic souls do not have a need to match a point of origin, so they are not created to be able to adjust their souls' inner tone or waveform. Even if they take physical form on any planet, they cannot change their inner tuning of tone enough to match that of the planet's harmonic tone. They are hardwired, so to speak, on the root waveform of the universal song and cannot make modifications to this tone. Their frequency can, and will, fluctuate with the energy that causes it. Remember, frequency and tone are different things.

The inability for dynamic souls to change their inner root tone, and the ability of static souls to make adjustments to the inner root tone is a great deal more important than you may think. It is it the key to tuning both your own toolbox, and thus your health; and the health of the entire planet you walk upon.

Since the earth node is a place where both tone and frequency are out of adjustment, there are none who live on her now, with either a static or dynamic soul, who are in harmonic agreement and free of frequency sickness.

Lesson 6
The Frequency of Life
part two

My dear child, before you page back through this book looking for part one of the lesson called "The Frequency of Life", please be aware that it is contained in the first book of lessons we shared together. If you are missing any of the prerequisite understanding for what is contained in this chapter, please refer to the first book of lessons for the missing information.

During this lesson and the next few as well, the tone and frequency we will be examining is that which can be considered the central tone or frequency found deep in the structure of your body and soul. General, physically based frequencies will be addressed in lesson 10. For now, let us focus on the physical cause of the frequency sickness of the earth by applying our new understanding as to how the dream was affected. To this end, let us move back in linear time to start our examination of the beginning of the frequency disruption as it occurred from a linear perspective. As you know from our previous lessons, the earth's natural tone and frequency has been corrupted over time by many different interlopers who came here and interfered with the natural course of life on this planet. By doing such things as mixing their own DNA with the earliest of mankind, they effectively created a race of human beings whom were not physically or tonally in tune with the earth.

Now that you are aware of the nature of static and dynamic souls, let us look into the simple explanation above with this new information in mind in order to help us understand how this mixing of DNA corrupted the human tone. This should also provide us with clues for how to rectify the tonal discord.

Before any interference, the earth held a tone and frequency that was in harmonic agreement with the universal song. The earth and eternity, if we can use a simple music analogy, were playing their notes in the same major chord. Just as the notes of a major chord, the notes will be different, but they are all harmonically compatible, and the sound they make when played together is agreeable. Everything on the earth shared the same tone as the earth, as well as the same frequency, which was not only the same as the earth, but also that of the universal song. In more metaphorical words, the Mother Earth and all parts of her had voices that sang in harmony with the universal song, and hearts that beat in time with the rhythm of that song.

This all changed the day a group of people from another world came to the earth. Of course, they came from a world that was not, itself, properly in tune with the universal song. For, indeed, child, if the interloper's home world were in harmony, they would not wish to leave it. In fact, it was because their own world was so out of tune and their own spiritual essence was so diluted, that this group of travelers saw no option but to find a new place to live.

If I may digress to an interesting piece of information you might wish to ponder, child; when spiritually based alternatives are invisible to those that seek to resolve the symptoms of frequency sickness, species often invent scientific methods to try to fix the problems. Inevitably, this leads to a growth in scientific knowledge as well as a growth in distance from the spiritual path to the correct answer, until all hope of a true resolution is lost. It is at about this time the species involved in the frequency sickness either uses its science to obliterate itself, or uses its science to find a way to travel to a new place and infect that place with its frequency discord. This is how the universal disease of frequency sickness travels from node to node. Moreover, child, if you ponder the way frequency sickness spreads from one node to another, and compare it to the actions of germs spreading from person to person, you can see it is another physical repeating expression.

Each group of beings to come to the earth had a mix of both static and dynamic souls among them. In fact, as in all cases, it was the dynamic souls among the group who were the ones central to the motivation needed to make the migration possible. Dynamic souls who enter physical life in places suffering extreme frequency discord, especially those who enter worlds where the spiritual ambition of the population is immature, will often lack a spiritual and energy based reason for their mission. Driven by a need to do something to help the people, but having no clue as to proper spiritual goals, they often become the leaders in migration or isolation plans, which only serve to strengthen or spread the frequency illness.

Be aware of this, and take a moment to recognize this could have happened to you. Congratulate yourself, child. You have not fallen into such a pitfall. This, in itself, child, is a wonderful accomplishment. To be able to grow and reach for spiritual enlightenment, while in a body suffering frequency sickness, living on a planet that is out of tune is nothing less than amazing. Take a moment to consider how few around you every day will even begin to understand that there is more to life than what fits in one's wallet. Now let us return to our lessons.

Bear in mind that dynamic soul beings have an unchanging direct agreement with the original universal tone, but their frequency is always different from the original frequency. Also remember that static soul beings will have a set frequency that is in direct agreement with that of the original universal frequency, but their inner tone will not be exactly the same as the original energy tone.

The interlopers who came to the Earth were not in tune with their own planet, and that planet itself was not in tune. We know this because static soul beings will keep a constant frequency with the dominant frequency that surrounds them in order to be in harmonic agreement with it. In the case of static soul beings, this dominant frequency should be the same as the universal song and the central frequency of the planet they live on. If the frequency of a static soul life form is not in line with the universal frequency, then it is proof that the planet on which they exist is not in agreement with that frequency and is in need of a tuning. Thus, it is easy to assume that any static soul beings who came to earth were carrying a disagreeable frequency that would upset anything on the earth it came in contact with.

We also know that dynamic soul beings were among those who came to the earth in physical form. Dynamic soul beings have a wide range of frequencies that can be adjusted with ease to a harmonic agreement when they embody themselves into a new physical container. But once in a container, they have the same limits on frequency adjustment as a static soul would. So, any dynamic soul beings that came to the earth would also have contributed to the offending frequency. Dynamic soul beings are not able to change their central tone, but their frequency changed easily to the offending vibration. This caused confusion to the energy direction of the planet itself. The frequency compromised earth was trying to vibrate to a central tone that was created to be in harmony with the universal song. Yet, due to the change in frequency, the tempo of the planet's song and the universal song were quickly moving out of the necessary synchronization. When you add in the influence of the strong central tone of the dynamic soul beings who interloped into the planet's energy sphere with their own version of the universal song, playing at its own pitch, you can imagine the frequency discord created.

The Mother Earth, being a resourceful being, tried to defend herself and regain her central tone. Consider for a moment the repeating expression you see in your own body when you catch a cold. Your body realizes it is being invaded by germs and sends out specialized cells to destroy the invading microbes. The Earth's body likewise created and sent out her own defenses, trying to get rid of the offending interlopers. She amended some of her natural resources, such as the bacteria she used to digest matter back into the soil, to attack the carriers of the invading tone. Unfortunately, it was not that simple. Much like some of the more insidious diseases man's body is subject to, the infestation changed so quickly and dramatically that the Mother Earth could not keep up her defenses. The final blow that occurs in almost all such scenarios happened here on earth. The interloping beings crossbred with the earth's natural population, mixing their DNA forever with that of the natural race.

You can think of DNA as a blueprint the universal force uses to create a physical container of something alive in the dream. DNA is, on a quantum level, the physical representation of the energy connection between the soul and the body on the primal physical level. Indeed, child, the quantum structure of DNA is made up of soul energy. If the soul that is to occupy a body is static in nature, this energy will come from the soul's own energy; if the soul is dynamic in nature, this energy will come from the node itself.

As with so many other worlds infected by frequency sick interlopers, the interlopers who visited the earth decided to interbreed with the earth life. The reason for this on earth varies, depending on which set of interlopers you refer to, but the reason why they intermixed is not important to this lesson. What is important is to understand that this mixing did take place.

Let us step back for a moment and examine what happens to the DNA of bodies housing static and dynamic souls on a tuned world. First, it must be understood, child, that when two physical beings copulate to create another life form, if they are successful, they only serve to create a physical container. Once the container is created, a soul will be attracted to it and will unite with it. The choice of what container a soul will inhabit will be based on many things. Often it is based in a strong spiritual memory of past existences with the parents. Such strong spiritual memories will draw people together lifetime after lifetime. Sometimes a container is chosen because it is in the correct place or situation. In such cases, a soul may be aware that he or she needs to be born into a certain place or time in order to do his or her work. In other cases, a soul may wish to be born into certain circumstances of strife or adversity in order to create a challenging growth opportunity. Other times a soul will be drawn to a particular container for no apparent reason, except perhaps because it suited Creation's need at the time.

When two beings of static souls procreate on a tuned world, the offspring they create will always be of a static soul in nature. In energy terms, when two harmonic tones with identical frequency combine, they create a physical container that is suited to house a static soul being. This melding of energy into a new physical form will attract the proper soul energy. Before very long, often before the physical shape of the container is more than just a few cells, a static soul unites with this physical shape and becomes one with it. This unity must happen in the very early stages of physical development when a static soul is involved, because some of the static soul's own energy has to become involved in the formation of the physical body. The earlier this happens, the easier the melding is. Since nature prefers an easy course, it comes natural for this to happen very early, even at the point of conception.

When two dynamic souls breed, the offspring they create will be, with very few exceptions, dynamic in nature. In energy terms, when two souls of universal tone agreement and varying frequency combine, they create a physical container that is suited to house a dynamic soul being. As above, the melding of the energy into a new physical form will attract the new soul to the container for the same reasons as stated above. That is, with one important exception. Dynamic souls do not come straight from Creation into a body, and they are not reincarnations of previous humans — although they may be re-embodiments of previous spirits who were once embodied as humans. Dynamic souls are always souls that come into physical life from the spirit realms. Since they are not designed to be fixed to a physical node, nothing of their own soul energy is used when creating the physical container, thus, they do not have to meld completely into the container at such a very early stage as a static soul would. Rather, the dynamic soul will naturally anchor only a part of itself to the physical body growing in the womb, and then create a small distance by engulfing the mother with his or her energy from the outside. This distance is important because the frequency of the dynamic soul is not always in harmony with the frequency of the raw matter of a physical node. The distance allows the dynamic soul time to adjust frequency to match that of the physical container. When the dynamic soul adjusts to a point of harmony with that which is natural to the physical container, the dynamic soul will naturally meld with that physical container and be one with it.

This usually happens within a month or so from conception, but in rare cases can take longer, particularly on a planet suffering from frequency sickness. It is during this delay in connection that the matrix of the physical container develops the part physical/part nonphysical links that will hold the soul to the body. None of the dynamic soul's energy is given to this process, as the dynamic soul is not embedded at the point when this takes place. Thus, it is the energy of the planet whose material essence is being used that will provide the material needed. This is why dynamic soul energy is not involved in the building of the connection between the physical and nonphysical when they take on corporeal form.

The earth-tone does not always step up right away and fill in the energy gap when a dynamic soul comes into the dream to incarnate. When this happens, the pregnancy will fail. For this reason, fertility rates are generally a bit lower for dynamic soul couples when compared to static soul couples.

On a properly tuned planet, if there were dynamic soul beings present in physical form and one did copulate for the purpose of reproduction with a static soul being, the child of their union would, with almost total certainty, have a static soul. This is because the static parents energy would be in total agreement with that of the planet, and this would create a strong energy draw to attract a static soul. In fact, on a planet where the tuning is never in question, 100% of the population will be static souls. Any dynamic souls who inhabit such planets do so in spirit form; or in other words, as energy beings.

Please understand, child, I am specifically referring to a planet that is sure to always tune positively or negatively for physical eternity when I say, "a planet where the tuning is never in question". Such planets do not suffer from the same type of frequency sickness in the same way that planets whose tunings are not assured do. Planets whose tunings are never in question have frequencies that must be adjusted, not because they changed or fell into discord, but rather because they are steady and not evolving, and therefore must be pushed up to the next harmonic level. This is truly more of an adjustment of tone, rather than a total tuning. This is why it is impossible for a dynamic and a static soul being to copulate and conceive a child on such a world. There would be no dynamic soul beings incarnate to take part in the copulation. That is, unless the dynamic soul being is an interloper on that world, which would put the planet's tuning in question, and void our example.

If, on the other hand, a planet whose tuning is in question comes to harmonic agreement and tunes with a population of dynamic soul beings already present, most of these dynamic soul beings will ascend back into spirit form and live on the planet as energy beings at the time of the tuning. Their work would be done and they would move on, thus not being part of the breeding cycle. Any dynamic soul beings who decided to remain in physical form in order to help with the newly tuned node, will already be in strong, unbreakable pair bonds with their completing dynamic soul reflections and will have no wish to procreate or even copulate with another. Any children dynamic soul beings create on a tuned world would be exempt from rule four and will come into the tuned world knowing who and what they are, and understanding what they are in physical form for. They will know better than to corrupt the frequency of the newly tuned world and would be mindful not to let the dynamic varying frequency corrupt the newly tuned static universal frequency. So we can see that on any tuned planet, there is really no chance of a dynamic soul being interbreeding with a static soul being and creating discord.

Please do not interpret this lack of mixing of frequencies between dynamic and static souls as any kind of race or class separation. It is not. Indeed, on tuned worlds where there are static and dynamic soul beings living together, there is absolutely no difference in their physical appearance, energy limits, soul understanding, or universal harmony. And indeed, they can, and do, bond together in extremely intimate ways that transcend that of a sexual coupling. It is just that on a tuned world, the creation of containers to be used by new souls entering the dream at that node is naturally controlled, as the people who live on these planets understand frequencies. I understand, child, this may seem strange or even a type of soul prejudice to you. But this is only because you cannot see beyond your limited view on a corrupted planet. If truth be told, child, on a planet in total harmony, it is as natural a thing as breathing, and is given as much contemplation and planning. After all, the strong central tone of the dynamic soul will be attracted to the identical tone in other dynamic souls. Likewise, the strong central frequency of the static soul will be drawn to souls of the same strong frequency. There will be no questions, no cross desires. It will be, as I said, as natural as breathing.

Here on earth, as on any planet that is in need of tuning, the story is different. Dynamic soul beings and static soul beings occasionally intermix. It is truly not a very common event, as static soul beings tend to be drawn together with static soul beings, and dynamic soul beings are likewise drawn together with dynamic soul beings. But it does happen from time to time.

When a dynamic soul beings and a static soul beings procreate on a planet which is out of tune and have offspring, the product of their union will most often be dynamic in nature at a ratio of about 70% over 30%. That is if conception happens and progresses to birth, which is not always assured. The reasons for this can seem complicated in its particulars. But in general terms, it can be explained as follows. Parents of different soul origins can attract both dynamic and static souls to the containers they create. Since the world they live on is out of tune, there is no added pull from the world's frequency to draw in static souls. The strong central tone of the dynamic soul parent then becomes a greater magnet, and the chance of attracting a dynamic soul to the container becomes more likely. The complication happens when the couple's energy attracts a dynamic soul, but the physical container their union creates is best suited for a static soul. Since the energy of the parents is split, the pull on the incoming spirit will be somewhat in conflict as it naturally tries to adjust to both of the parents soul state. When this happens, if the incoming soul cannot overcome the difference and embed itself in the container, the pregnancy will fail.

Add to this the concern about the planet stepping in and filling in the connecting energy and the overall fertility rate will go down. Nevertheless, for offspring who are born, the majority will be dynamic soul beings by nature, simply because of the strong attractive force of the dynamic soul parent.

Over time, more and more children are being born who have dynamic souls, which is good for the mission and good for you, dear one. For it is from these dynamic souls the bulk of the tuning workforce will come. For it is truly only dynamic soul beings who can perform the work necessary to bring about the tuning. But I am jumping ahead of our lessons, child. Let us return to the exploration of how this node, earth, became so corrupted.

Knowing what you now know about dynamic and static soul types, you can imagine the disruption that can take place when the source for the energy that makes up the DNA of a person from another planet intermixes with the DNA of a person on a tuned world. This is exactly what has happened on earth. In order to fix these disruptions, you must have an understanding of how they work.

Let us assume, for the sake of argument, that there is a tuned planet called planet A. This planet has a dominant life form on it that follows the basic repeating expression common in the physical universe in which it resides, that being a dominant, bipedal, mammalian, sentient life. Let us also assume that there is a planet B in this same universe. Due to the law of repeating expression, planet B also has a dominant, sentient, bipedal, mammalian life form living on it. Unfortunately, planet B is not in tune. The planetary frequency and tone, as well as the frequency and tone inherent in the dominant race, is out of agreement with the universal order.

Now, let us assume that for reasons unimportant to this example, the people on planet B launch an expedition to planet A. The individuals in this expedition are a mix of beings, some with static souls and some with dynamic souls. They arrive on planet A, and in a short time, decide to intermix their DNA with the dominant life form on Planet A.

What happens next? First, let us look at the type of disruption the crossbreeding of static souls from different planets causes. As you know, static soul beings resonate with the vibrational tone of the planet of their origin. A being from planet A would have an identical tone to that of his tuned world. That tone would be in harmonic agreement with the universal tone. The frequency of the being, the planet, and the Creation Force would be identical.

Now let us consider the interloper from planet B. As a static soul, one may be tempted to assume that the interloper from planet B would carry a planetary tone that is in harmonic agreement with the universal tone, thus in harmonic agreement with planet A. One may even venture to assume that since all static soul beings have an identical frequency that matches the universal song exactly, that static soul beings from any world would be in frequency agreement with any other static soul being. Indeed, if planet B was also tuned, both these assumptions would be correct. But we know that if any being wishes to leave the planet on which he originates, than he is clearly not in tune. Therefore, it must be assumed that planet B is not in tune and the people who come from planet B are likewise not in tune.

If it were possible that the expedition from planet B was comprised of just static soul based beings, and that planet B had only static tone disruption, then when the beings from planet B mixed their DNA with that of the people on planet A, the offspring would be people who have a tone between that of the tuned planet A parent and the tainted planet B parent. Yet, there is still the chance that if the frequency of planet B is not corrupted, that at least the frequency of the offspring would still be in tune.

If there are any dynamic soul beings involved in the intermixing of DNA, which there are sure to be as dynamic soul beings will always be the driving force for such expeditions, then the damage of the interlopers is going to be much worse. Consider this scenario. If a dynamic soul being from planet B were to mix DNA with a being from planet A, the offspring would have a frequency that is no longer the same as that of the planet or the universal song. And even though the central tone of a dynamic soul being is in harmonic agreement with planet A, it cannot come down to that of planet A and will not mesh well with the physical form which life takes on planet A.

When you compound this with the understanding that no beings, static or dynamic in soul nature, who come to planet A are in tune to begin with, it becomes clear that the offspring of such unions will be something quite different from what the planet requires. Once these primary energies are corrupted, the corruption will spread without the need for procreation. The hybrid frequencies and tones are close enough to that of the natural life on the planet that just by their presence, these energies will subtly mold and change the tones and frequencies around them, until the corruption is wide spread.

As these children of corrupted frequency and tone intermix, they spread the faulty DNA structure to their offspring, that in turn, spread it to greater extents. The more individuals affected by the discord, the more the balance of planet A becomes one of discord. Eventually, the balance ends up in the favor of discord and planet A is forced to try and adjust to the new discord. Planet A is required to try to adapt her own tone and frequency into agreement with the overall consensus of the beings that live on her. As she does this, she also starts to defend herself by sending out germs and other sickness carrying creations to try and destroy the beings with the offending frequency and tone.

When the first race of interlopers came to the earth and intermixed their DNA with that of the true Earthers, frequency sickness was spread to the earth. But this was only the beginning. As time passed, the frequency discord of the earth attracted other beings from other frequency sick worlds to the earth, and they added their own discord to the earth-song. Even to this day, with all the precautions that are in place to stop the future corruption of the DNA code of the Earthers, it continues. Not only at the hands of beings from other worlds, but indeed, child, mankind is so confused, that he is hard at work every day destroying his own DNA with everything from random chemical exposure to deliberate DNA tampering by way of gene research.

This leads me to another interesting and important tangent. Child, never eat genetically altered food. Science and the commercial market have come together in recent years to create genetically altered food by changing the genetic code of the food. These foods are very bad for you. Even those that seem to be quite healthy are not. In fact, they could be quite harmful to your soul energy and even deadly to your body. Today, mankind has been tampering with the DNA in all kinds of food. They have created cows with genetic codes to make their meat more marbled and tender, to tomatoes that do not bruise easily. Indeed, every year more and more genetically altered food reaches your grocery stores each day. Avoid such foods.

Please be aware that this does not apply to naturally crossbred or hybrid foods. Plants and animals that can naturally be hybridized without laboratory based intervention are not considered genetically altered. For example, if a farmer pollinates one type of apple tree with the pollen of another type of apple tree and produces a hybrid apple, this hybrid apple is not altered in a harmful way. Likewise, if a farmer houses two different breeds of chicken together and they naturally produce young, the offspring are not considered genetically altered. If two types of animals or plants can produce the next generation by natural exposure, then this is not harmful.

Unnatural, and thus frequency harming, genetic altering occurs when either two plants or animals are crossbred in a way that could not naturally happen without the intervention of mankind's technology, or when the actual DNA coding is tampered with in a laboratory. Stay away from any food source that has been tampered with and genetically altered. No matter how fresh it looks, no matter how nutritious it is said to be, genetically altered food is frequency sick food.

Let us return to our lesson, child. As you are aware, the earth has been tainted by several races of beings with their own tones and frequencies. Each of these races came from a frequency sick planet and each has spread its own type of infection to the earth and its residents. There are several distinct pockets of very different types of frequency sickness on the earth, as well as an overall sickness. Some of these pockets are due to the relative isolation a tainted population lived in until recent years. Other concentrated pockets are due to the grouping of people with like frequencies gathering together.

The good news is, child, that it is not important to know whose invading tone did what damage in order to sort it all out. If you noticed, once enough people were out of tune with the earth, the earth adjusted its tone to try and find a point of agreement. This is important because it means that when enough people start working on correcting their own frequency and tone problems, the earth will sooner or later follow suit and bring its own frequency and tone up to find agreement. When this happens, the tuning is not far behind.

Lesson 7

The Frequency of Life
part three

It is more important for your personal growth and awakening to understand the results of frequency sickness from a spiritual point of view. This can be best achieved by having an idea of what it would be like on a world of no frequency sickness, and comparing this to the world today. Yes, child, you may assume everything would be in harmony. But what exactly does that mean? What would a day on a planet without frequency sickness be like?

Well, child, as you can imagine, it would be quite bit different from where you are today. Even if you were to strip all hate, fear, evil, and sin from your world; even if you were to remove every seedy bar, every crack house, and any other unpleasant symptom of societal frequency sickness, it would still be different from what you are apt to imagine.

Indeed, child, you may be surprised that in a world free from frequency sickness, there is very little in the way of technology. There are no big cities or buildings. There are no streets paved with gold, or the mines required to dig out that gold. There are no cars to drive on those roads if they did exist. In a tuned world, all sentient life is in harmony with nature and the planet. The world takes care of them, and they take care of the world in return. There is no violence because there is no discord. There is growth through creative processes, not through painful friction. Love is the dominant frequency and compassion is the tool that is used to show that frequency. Though sickness is not necessary, there is still life and death. Both life and death are understood and accepted for what they are.

Happiness on a tuned world has nothing to do with what you own. It has nothing to do with what you can do better than your neighbor. It has only to do with the part of Creation you are and how you interact with other parts of that Creation.

The lion may lie down with the lamb in biblical heaven, but on the tuned world, nature will still have a food chain like it does now. Unlike here on earth, all predators will be grateful to the souls of the things they consume. This includes predators of plants as well as those who eat other animals. After all, physical life is structured in this way. It will be on a tuned world as well. The difference is that on a tuned world it is understood and respected.

As you can see, you are not living on a tuned world, child. Even in the simplest of sense, you are probably out of spiritual sync with what would happen on a tuned world. For example, you may have found the habit of saying a prayer of thanks to God or Creation for giving you your dinner. But how many of you, child, take the time to thank the sweet peas and lettuce by name for giving their life force to you?

On a tuned world, the sweet peas would never be forgotten for giving up their life so you could live. In addition, on a tuned world, you would be sure to plant more sweet peas with the intention that you are creating a way to return the life force you took away from the sweet peas. You would not only nurture these new seeds and plants with water, you would take time each day to share some of your own energy with them to help them grow. This is quite a bit different from the reason you would plant sweet peas in today's world.

You may be tempted to say that the results are the same. But, in fact, child, they are very different. When you thank the sweet peas for the energy they sacrificed to you, and you nurture their seeds and new plants with your own energy as they grow anew, you create a harmony between you and the sweet peas that enriches both you and the sweet peas on a deeply spiritual level. In the end, rather than just having food for your body, you have a partnership with another life form that also feeds your frequency and reinforces your connection to your world and Creation.

Even today, on this mistuned earth, if you take the time to understand that your food is giving its own life force to you, and you are sincerely thankful for this, you will see that your food will digest better and even be more nutritious for your body. If you garden, spend some time every day projecting your energy to your plants, and you will notice a marked difference in the plants overall health, and the size, flavor, and spiritual energy you gain from each meal.

On a tuned planet, people will be born, grow, live, and die, just like on the earth, but they will do it in a natural and truly communal way. Birth will be a rejoicing as a new soul enters the community journey. Childhood will be filled with learning and growing, playing and loving. Adults will continue the joys of childhood long into their senior years. Growth will stem from playing, loving, creating art, music, and other joy building activities. Families will be extended, with whole villages related to some degree. Sickness will be unknown, but death will still be at the end of life's journey. Death will be understood as a natural part of the physical experience. After all, there is little point in experiencing physical life, if you never bring that experience back to Creation. The harmony with true Creation beyond the dream will be a palpable comfort. Everyone on the planet will be on the same frequency, quite literally, and each will feel united with every other. The examples could go on and on.

As you can see, the earth is far from in tune. But this does not mean that she will stay this way. Indeed, she must change, and change soon. When you look around yourself, it is easy to see that a lot will change between now and the tuning of the earth. You may be tempted to think that there will have to be terrible destruction of whole cities and countries in order to wipe out the metropolis around you. You may have come to believe, or other teachers may have even told you, that times of great devastation must happen before the earth can find her balance. Many people think that the only way the earth can return to a natural paradise is by way of a grand worldwide conflagration that will destroy all remnants of mankind's cities and technology. But indeed, child, they are all wrong.

When the Mother Earth tunes, her very nature will change to match the consensus of the aware who live on her. Quite literally, the *thoughts* of the aware will change the reality of the earth in less than a heartbeat. Do you find this hard to believe, dear child? If you do, then perhaps you have forgotten. Thought is GOD. Thus, child, the spiritual aspect of the tuning could be justly thought of as the attention of the God Force returning to the Earth in order to correct her frequency and tone.

The return of a God figure to fix the earth is a rather common theme for those familiar with the doctrine of any formal religion. Yet, as you can see, child, the interpretation given by such religions to the most basic fact that God will fix the earth is significantly obtuse when compared to the truth, that the *thoughts of God* in physical form will change the earth. That is, once they know what they are and what they are here to do.

You are here to tune the planet. The planet is the largest physical object you will ever encounter. Yet, the Mother Earth herself has a soul. The Mother Earth's soul wants to find her tune. She wants to get well, but she is helpless to cure herself without help at this point, since the frequency sickness has spread so far and so fast. This said, it is important to know that the soul of the Mother Earth is not totally helpless. She is willing to help those who are working to tune her. Unfortunately, few, if any of you, child, have the ability to converse with the her in such a direct way as to let the her know you are on her side. Your actions are not distinguishable from any other human's. She does not know if you are recycling. She does not know if you are planting trees. She does not even know if you are not the one who is digging out her magnetic heart. This is why she attacks you with her germs.

The only way to tell the Mother Earth you are not the enemy, and thus save yourself from many of the germs and illnesses out there that make your life uncomfortable, at best, or could end your life, at worse, is to project the proper frequency signal. This can only be done by working on your central spiritual frequency.

Your spiritual frequency is the vibrational rhythm that you were first given when you departed from the central Creation Force. For a static soul being, this vibration started off as identical to that of the one universal song. For dynamic souls, this vibration started off as a harmonic interval to that of the one universal song. Either way, the frequency you began with would have been in harmonic agreement with the earth, and thus, not perceived as harmful by the earth in a tuned situation.

The central frequency of the soul — that is, the frequency set when the soul entered the dream — is corrupted on a planet that has a tainted tune. Since it is this central frequency the planet recognizes in order to judge what is part of her and what is not, it is this frequency that must change in order for people to be mostly free from germs, shadow people, and other forms of earthly defense mechanisms.

There is one catch. The Mother Earth herself is so out of tune that even if you are able to tune your own central frequency to your original frequency, you will still not be in tune with the earth. You would be in a closer harmonic range, and you would surely benefit, but you would never be totally free from germs. This is the reason why the plants and animals on the earth who have not suffered any frequency interloping are still subject to germs and illness. It is not because they are out of tune, it is because their properly tuned frequency no longer matches the frequency of the sick earth.

So, if the earth is no longer tuned, and even those animals that have a natural frequency that has not been tampered with cannot find true harmonic agreement with her, what hope is there for any of you, child? This is a good question. The answer is hidden in the paradox that tells us that a dynamic soul can never be in total frequency agreement with a node; and indeed, dynamic souls are always the cause of frequency sickness. Yet, it is only dynamic souls who can truly tune a planet. How? The key to the answer is in the central tone of the dynamic soul. Keep this in mind for lesson 9, The Tuning: part two.

Lesson 8
Of the Spiritual Body
part two

Again, child, I must reference you to our first book of lessons. This is where you will find, *Of the Spiritual Body*. If any of the information in this chapter is based on concepts you do not understand as of yet, please review the corresponding lesson in the first book.

As you know, child, your physical self has three distinct parts. You have a physical body, an astral body, and a light body. In addition to all of these bodies, you have layers of energy that bind these parts of your body together in a spiritual or energy sense. These binding parts are often referred to as your aura and your energy sheathe. The aura is the layer of energy between the physical and the astral body. The energy sheathe is the layer between the astral body and the light body. Both are important parts of the total of your being and both need to be considered when we look deeper into the workings of the spiritual body. Let us explore what they are, how to discover them, and how to glean information from each.

The aura, as you probably already know, child, is an energy field that surrounds a physical body. It is often described as being made of different colors. Many sensitive individuals can, if the conditions are right, see auras and will describe them in terms of colors. Indeed, there are some people who can see auras who do not know it because rather than seeing color, they see distortion of light, haze, or other such indications which they often disregard. Under certain conditions, when proper electric fields are projected through the human body and charge the aura body, the aura can even be photographed — almost. That is to say, that the photographs show the effect of the electric impulses that are projected through the aura.

The aura is always changing as one experiences emotions or moves closer or further away from a higher state of consciousness. The aura is very much like a soul thermometer. When one is in touch with the workings of the aura, one can use the information the aura presents for many uses. Healing and consoling are the two uses most commonly applied by those whom can see or feel the auras of others. These are good practices. Nevertheless, there are few who know how to work with their own aura to correct frequency discord and to heal the connection between their physical and spirit bodies.

If you believe you cannot see your own aura, there are several ways you can learn to do so. They all take time and practice, as everything does, but they are worth the while. Let us, child, start with the method most will find successful.

Start by sitting in a comfortable place. Do not pick a busy place. If this place can be outdoors, it is even better, as you will not be surrounded by as much interfering frequency. If you have access to still water, you can use this as a reflective pool, otherwise, hold or place a mirror out of the direct line of the sun, in such a way that you can see most of your body, or at least your head and shoulders. Take several deep calming breaths and clear your mind of any cluttering thoughts. Look at yourself in the mirror. Do your best not to blink too often. Do not move or speak. After a short time, you are likely to see the contours of your face change. Do not be startled, this is expected. Allow it to happen. Soon after this change, you will begin to see colors around your reflection. This is your aura.

Another way to see at least part of your aura is to meditate on your hand. Hold your hand in front of you as you meditate. As you slip into a higher state, you will begin to see the aura around your hand. If you are careful not to bring your state down, you can then look over your whole body to see what your aura looks like on other parts.

To see another person's aura, have the person sit in strong daylight against a white background. Raise your state of being while looking at the person. Try not to blink too often. Do not move or talk if you do not have to. After a short while, you will begin to see a color around your subject. This will be the aura.

Once you have developed the ability to see auras, and you begin to use this ability, it will come with such ease that you will no longer have to work at it.

What is the importance of seeing auras? When you see your own aura, child, or that of another person, you will be able to judge the condition of the frequency that binds the physical body to the astral. This will say a lot, for it is a very accurate indicator of the physical frequencies held in a body. This makes it a powerful tool for adjusting the frequency of your own body and anyone else you choose to apply your skills to.

As you know, child, you are surrounded by negative frequency every day. It is in everything from your food to the air you breath. Some of these frequencies will move through you with little problem. But many will stick in your body, affecting certain parts of your body, causing all kinds of frequency sickness. Examining the aura is like taking an MRI of the frequencies in the body.

Even more important than the aura to frequency health, is the layer between the astral and the light body. This layer is called, in our lessons, the energy sheathe. It should not be confused with the Hindu concept of psychic sheath or manomaya kosa. Unlike the psychic sheath of yoga, the energy sheathe is not limited. In truth, the energy sheathe of the human body is the last part of the body that has any direct physical connection to the earth illusion. It is, for all intents and purposes, best described as the layer of glue that holds the physical aspects of your body to your nonphysical light body. For, remember, child, as we learned in our first lesson on the spiritual body, your astral body has a physical presence.

As you may surmise, child, since it is the glue that holds physical to nonphysical, it will differ in composition for a static and dynamic soul type. This is true. In fact, child, a static soul being's energy sheathe is such that it could hardly be thought of as separate from the static soul being's light body, or higher self.

As we know, static soul beings are connected directly to their physical bodies via their own energy. That energy comes from their light body. In other words, static souls are connected to the physical by the energy of their own soul.

Dynamic soul beings, on the other hand, cannot use any of their light being in order to connect to physical bodies. A dynamic soul being needs to use energy from another source. In the case of dynamic soul beings on earth, that source is the earth's own energy. Since the earth's energy is not part of the dynamic soul being's spirit — higher self or light body — the energy sheathe is a distinct and separate layer of the being. And, as you might imagine, it is an extremely important part, as it makes it possible for the dynamic soul being to enter into physical form.

The energy sheathes of both dynamic and static souls cannot be seen with the eyes, except perhaps by a very limited number of individuals; not more than a handful worldwide. It can only be felt with the psychic senses. Interestingly, it is not difficult to train sensitive individuals to sense energy sheathes.

The energy sheathe is susceptible to different discord depending on the type of soul it belongs to. Static soul being's energy sheathes will be affected by central *frequency* discord only. If the central soul frequency of the static soul being is not in complete agreement with the true universal song, as given from the pure Creation source, then the energy sheathe will be compromised. The extent of the damage is wholly dependent on the vibration of the discord. Likewise, only one thing can hurt the energy sheathe of a dynamic soul. That is, child, if the central soul *tone* of the dynamic soul being is not in complete agreement with the true universal song, as given from the pure Creation source.

Regardless of what type of soul a physical being possesses, any damage to the energy sheathe will cause a state of disconnect between the physical body, intellect and awareness, and the light body or the higher spiritual self. The greater the damage, the greater the gap will be.

The method used to teach a person to *see* his or her energy sheathe is also one method a person can use to verify if they have a dynamic or static soul. Although it must be noted that if a person is even remotely interested in seeing his or her energy sheathe, then he or she is, beyond almost all doubt, a dynamic soul. Nevertheless, both results will be explored in this lesson.

Again, I must note that you are not going to be actually looking at your energy sheathe during this exercise, as it cannot be seen. Rather, you will be doing what the electricity does when photographing an aura. You will be sending energy through your energy sheathe and experiencing the resulting reaction. This is how it is done.

Work yourself into state where your mind is quiet and your body is still. Take several deep breaths. With each breath, imagine that you are inhaling pure light energy. Do not let this energy exit when you exhale. Hold the feeling of the energy inside your body, almost like holding your breath. But do not hold your breath. With each new breath you should be feeling a bit more full of energy. For some this will feel like a sort of muscle tension. For others it might feel like a growing urge to move. Some may feel a growing calm. Regardless of the sensation, you should begin to sense a fullness or build up of energy in your body. Continue to do this until your body seems to be full to bursting with energy. When it seems like you are reaching the limit of the amount of energy you can inhale, put your hands upon your solar plexus and push the built up energy through it.

If done correctly, you should experience a burst of energy in your body through your solar plexus. The reaction for a dynamic soul being will feel much like the energy is moving from the center of your body and up, then through your body, and perhaps even continuing out of your body. For a static soul being, the feeling will remain localized in the center of the body.

Take careful note of the feeling that spreads through the body. When the energy sheathe is intact and healthy, the energy will feel pleasant, if not invigorating. If there is any sense of pain, nausea, or depression, then the energy sheathe is damaged and needs to be attended too.

It is very likely, child, that your energy sheathe is not badly damaged, if it is damaged at all. I can say this with some certainty because you are working on your spiritual growth. Dynamic soul beings who have greatly damaged energy sheathes do not have any incentive to work on their spiritual growth. Indeed, child, they will have little idea that they have a spiritual life at all. It is interesting to note, that since static soul beings, in general, are not naturally spiritually based workers by design, the damage of their energy sheathes does not stop them from pursuing any type of religious goals they may hold in their life. Rather, a static soul being with a damaged energy sheathe will exhibit symptoms of moral distortion. The greater the damage, the greater their morally distorted views will manifest in their words and deeds. Just look at the doers of senseless violence in this world and you will see static soul beings that have extremely damaged energy sheathes.

Energy sheathes, regardless of the owner's soul type, can only be harmed when the central frequency or tone is not in agreement with that of the true universal frequency or tone. This is an important thing to know. There are many, many frequencies and tones around you every day. And although these frequencies and tones can harm you in various ways, the tones and frequencies of every day life, in and of themselves, cannot harm your energy sheathe. It is only severe, repeated or prolonged bombardment by the same invading, extremely low frequency or tone that will damage the energy sheathe. This extremely low frequency or tone can come from the environment; such as when a person lives with, or is surrounded by, others with such frequency. It can come from music and other media; such as when a person is consistently exposed to the malicious frequencies hidden in some music, TV shows, or movies. It can, on rare occasions, come from the influences of negatively motivated spirits who interpose themselves into a person's life. But this last occurrence is rare. By far, negative entities are attracted by energy sheathe damage, rather than being the cause of it.

The healing of the energy sheathe is an important part of creating a strong, spiritually motivated force in your life. When your energy sheathe is whole and undamaged, your psychic and empathic senses will be at their best. Your emotions will be more stable and your capacity for compassion will be limitless. More important than even these significant benefits, when your energy sheathe is whole, your inner soul is in pure harmonic agreement with the true universal tone of the Creation Force. Having as healthy and whole an energy sheathe as you can manage is essential to your work in tuning the planet. You will see why in lesson 9, The Tuning: part two.

So, child, you now know you have an aura and energy sheathe in addition to your physical body, astral body, and light body. You also know how to examine your aura and your energy sheathe. Now you need to learn how to interpret what you observed and how to make the proper adjustments as needed. We will begin with the aura.

The aura is seen by most as a pattern of colors. These colors are the brain's way of perceiving certain frequency patterns given off by an aura. The colors of the aura are often misunderstood. Indeed, there are so many different ways of interpreting what each color means, that if you look long enough, you will find someone that will tell you that a certain color means exactly the opposite of what another will tell you that color means.

It is important to note that the analysis of color frequencies in objects and physical things around you is totally different from the analysis of color in the aura. For example, the red in a bright rose carries a frequency of healing. The red in an aura, on the contrary, indicates a low vibrational tone often associated with physical illness or emotional pain. The darker to black the red, the more inflamed the infection or deep the emotional pain. Keep this in mind as we explore what the colors of your aura mean. Also, keep in mind, that we will only be addressing that which involves the work to balance frequency sickness with the primary aim of adjusting central frequency and tone, and by no means does this lesson encompass all that can be learned or known from examining the aura.

When talking about frequency sickness and how it manifests in the aura, one has to recall our lesson on what frequency is. The two points that bear review at this time are that frequency is the number of times a waveform repeats itself in a given segment of time; and higher frequencies are closer to the true eternal tone of Creation because they include more perfect waveforms, and thus are more positive in nature. With this in mind, let us talk about the nature of color.

Color is simply the human brain's way of decoding a certain type of frequency of light that enters through the eye. When you see your aura, you see colors because your brain finds that the frequencies given off by aura energy are closest in relation to the type of waves given off by physical color. Aura energy colors, like colors of light waves, follow a certain pattern, with one exception. When you look at a color with your eyes, you are not seeing the object project the color. Rather, you are seeing only the waves of color frequency that are reflected off that object. A rose is not red because it is projecting red light from within. A rose is red because it is absorbing all other bands of light except red, which it reflects back at your eyes.

On the other hand, child, the colors you see when you look at your aura are being perceived on a psychic level, and not on a physical level. When you see a color in your aura, it is there because the aura is emitting it, not because it is reflecting it.

Colors, as you know, are forms of frequency. Aura emitted colors are not visible to the eye, but rather perceived psychically. Because they are similar to color waves the brain is used to, with practice, it will learn to convert them to what appears to be visible color by the brain. The frequency of each color is about the same as it would be in the physical world. Thus, reds have the longer waveforms and lower frequencies; and violets have the shorter waveforms and higher frequencies. This means, as you may assume, that the closer to violet an aura color is, the better. This is true because the higher the frequency, the closer to the Creation energy that frequency is.

Auras are often made up of several colors that usually extend for several feet beyond the physical body. If you have ever had a stranger stand too close to you, making you feel like your personal space was invaded, you know what it feels like to have the aura of the uninvited touch your own. Do not be concerned if you only see aura colors on or very close to your body when you view your aura. It is not important that you see the extent of your aura to know it is there.

When you look at your aura colors, or, indeed, the auras of any others, you will see various colors around various energy points of the body. If you see any concentrated red spots, be mindful that this usually means that a part of your body in the area of the spot may be physically ill. Most people you will meet will have auras that lean towards the color range that starts at yellow and moves up to green. Without going into any long and unnecessary explanation as to what these colors mean, what you need to know, child, is that red, orange, and yellow are far to low in frequency for you to work effectively on your spiritual goals. And though these colors might suit most static souls quite well, you are likely to feel physically sick and mentally depressed when your aura is mostly made up of these colors. Green is a good beginning place for you to be. It is a neutral color, energy wise, when it comes to auras. Any color above green, such as blue, indigo, and violet are where you truly will feel the best, and will work the best.

If I may lead you on another tangent at this point, since the topic of aura colors and indigo has come up, it is a good time to tell you a little bit about the phenomena of indigo children. Perhaps you are the parent of an indigo child, or you are one yourself. You are likely to know that since the time of tuning is coming near, many dynamic souls have come into physical form at this time to help with the effort. This wave of new dynamic souls can often be identified by the brilliant indigo color that dominates their aura. Indigo children are smart, sensitive, and usually quite psychic from an early age.

There is one important thing about indigo children that has been greatly and dangerously overlooked by the population who parent them and teach them. It is this. When such a flood of adept souls suddenly choose to take physical form on a certain node, it is a sure sign that a tuning is imminent. It is also sure to attract the attention of the beings whose intentions are to make the tuning a negative one. These negative beings will follow the indigo children, and, if given the chance, will take advantage of their compromised position as children to work their way into the child's being. Many parents of indigo children are told that it is only natural for indigo children to march to their own drummers, since they have an inner knowledge they follow. And this is the truth. But often parents and teachers of indigo children are made to believe that they must ignore or even encourage any negative or antisocial behavior on the part of their child, under the umbrella excuse that indigo children are destined to be unruly. This is a dangerous way of thinking with an indigo child.

Indigo children are a strong energy lure for negative beings. Often, beings of dark intent will work to befriend an indigo child in order to pull him or her away from a great destiny. This is particularly true when the child reaches teen years and feels the need to create a distance from the parents.

If the indigo child is raised without limits or rules from an early age, they are primed to fall victim. The indigo children at the greatest risk are those whose parents are so focused on their own issues and growth that they do little or no true parenting, particularly when the children are young. Also at risk are the indigo children of parents who do not have any structure in their own life, and thus, cannot give any to their children. Indigo children in such environments will become very rebellious. The rebellion is rooted in a power struggle. Since the parents have not given the child any powerful structure to his or her early years, when the child comes into adolescence and begins to sense his or her own personal power, the child will confront the parents that are then perceived as weaker and not worthy of respect. In such cases, the unruly nature of the child, confronting adults with meager parenting skills, inevitably leads to the unnecessary medicating of the child.

Of course, this is true with any children, not just indigo children. But, when the child is an indigo, this quickly develops into an extremely perilous problem. Such frequency discourse opens the way for negative spirits to be accepted by the indigo. This is not to say that the indigo will openly let the evil thing into his or her life, but thoughts of anger and resentment from such psychic beings, as well as the frequency fouling effects of the medications often given to such children, will allow the negative entity to enter into the indigo child's life, energy, and even body. Once this happens, the indigo child will become extremely unruly or seriously depressed. What was once natural childhood rebellion and need for structure, will quickly devolve into something truly negative and harmful in nature, that presents itself both inwardly and outwardly, destroying the hopes, goals, and abilities of the spirit that is the indigo child.

Why do I sidetrack our lessons into such a tangent, you may be asking yourself. I do this because indigo children and their auras are a perfect example of what you need to know when reading your own aura. You see, when you look at the aura of an indigo child, you should find that the dominant color of the aura is a beautiful deep purple blue. By deep, I mean rich in color, not dark. If the indigo is mixed with black, it is an indication of frequency sickness. If it is very dark, especially if it is almost black, it is a clear indication that something of negative influence is interacting with the child's energy body. All aura colors should be bright, even if they are deep and rich. This is true for indigo children and it is true for you as well.

When you look at your aura, be mindful of any dark spots you see. A deep purple is wonderful, a blackish purple is not. Likewise, a deep blue is wonderful, a black blue is not. Light shades of blues and purples are good. Rich, bright colors are best.

The first thing to do when you view your aura is to take note of any colors that appear to be mixed with black. Note where on your aura they are. Dark colors are frequency sick colors and must be adjusted. If there are blacks or near blacks in your aura color, you need to do work on a spiritual cleaning before you work on your frequency. Truly, child, it is not likely you will see anything near black, because it is not likely you have much, if any, true evil attached to you at this point in your spiritual development. But in the event that you do see black in your aura, or you have an indigo child who has a dark aura, there are several ways to move the dark thing from your life. The easiest and most effective method is to give it the gift of true unconditional love. Visualize the dark thing. Then visualize it engulfed in universal love. Understand in your heart that all things, including negative things, are a necessary part of the growth of Creation. Thank the thing for doing its part in the plan of Creation and project your unconditional love towards it. Your positive frequency will be like a tuning fork on the teeth to the source of the darkness and it will go away.

When you look at your own aura and you see an abundance of colors in the red to yellow range, then you know that your frequency needs to be raised. It is not hard to raise your aura frequency. Since aura frequencies are much like color, color can be effective in helping you raise your aura frequency. It is simply a matter of moving up the rainbow.

Let us say that your aura presents itself with predominant yellow. Think of the colors of the rainbow: Red, orange, yellow, green, blue, indigo, violet. The next color you will want to reach up to will be the next in the rainbow. In this case you will want to reach for green. Using green as an example, let us explore how to reach for a color to adjust the aura. The first thing you want to do is find some object that has a deep, rich shade of green. Be sure it is a bright rich green, like in the rainbow. Also, be sure it is a shade of green that you like. By this, child, I do not intend for you to pick a color you think looks good on you, or matches your eyes. I mean, rather, choose a color that makes you feel happy to look at. Do not pick something that is dark green, bordering on black. Place the object where you can see it and mediate on the object often. As you do, visualize absorbing or even drinking the color into your aura. I frequently tell my students to envision their aura as being made of sponge, and the color they focus on as being made out of liquid. Then I instruct them to envision the aura sponge absorbing the liquid color. It may take several tries over several days to make the connection to the new color. You do not have to spend hours in meditation if you do not have the time. Even a minute here or there throughout the day will be helpful. Every minute you are working on tuning your aura to the new color, you are tuning your aura and energy to a higher frequency. Every day or so check your aura again to see if the new color is taking effect. Besides your aura, you should sense the changing frequency in your body as you go along.

You may be tempted to jump right to the top of the spectrum and focus on violet, but this is not a good idea unless you are at a firm, bright, rich indigo. Never jump ahead more than one color or frequency at one time. You want to make a permanent change in your aura energy. If you jump too far, too fast, you will only find yourself bouncing back to your lower color range over and over again.

Once the majority of your aura colors appear in the blue range the majority of the time, your aura frequency is in an acceptable range for working on other frequencies.

Please be aware, child, that the colors of your aura will change from moment to moment. Every emotion you experience will cause subtle changes to the hue and value of the colors you will see. Physical sickness and emotional upset will send your aura colors into a shamble. When you look at your aura for adjustment, do not judge your results on one reading. Rather, use an overall assessment of the dominant color over time. Even if your normal aura colors are predominately violet, your aura may appear a wash of red when you are emotionally stressed or physically ill. Such things are temporary conditions and do not cause negative overall effects so long as the majority of the time your aura colors are in the blue or better frequency range.

Once the aura is in a good energy range, you will find that your psychic awareness will increase. You will get better sleep. Your health will improve. The energies around you will become more positive. Unlucky events and unkind people will no longer be an issue, as they will no longer be attracted to your aura energy. And most of all, you will be in a strong solid position to heal the frequency sickness you suffer because of the world around you.

The healing of your energy sheathe is not as straightforward as the healing of the aura. Your energy sheathe is not something that you can willfully adjust with simple frequency adjustments. Your energy sheathe is something that is affected — positively or negatively — by the things around you and the thoughts those things inspire in you. Surround yourself with negative people, negative frequencies, and negative visions, and you will cause damage to your energy sheathe. This is especially true if you do nothing to counteract the negative influences around you. Likewise, your energy sheathe is healed by surrounding yourself with positive people, positive frequencies, and positive visions.

Since the energy sheathe is the part of your total body that is the bridge between the parts of you that are physically in the dream and your higher spirit self, it is the part of your body that is skilled at physical manifestation. Thus, it is the part that is called into action when you invoke higher agreement — often called the law of attraction, which you do with every breath you take. The stronger and healthier your energy sheathe, the more powerful you will find your skills are to create your own reality and physically and spiritually affect the dream.

Lesson 9
The Tuning
part two

At this point, child, I would like to make what might appear to be a diversion in the unfolding of our lessons and talk about the tuning. We will return to our discussion about the energy sheathe and individual frequency healing soon.

As with the lesson entitled, *Frequency of Life:* part one, the lesson entitled, *The Tuning* part one, can be found in our first volume of lessons together. If you have not read it, or if it has been some time since you have reviewed it, you may wish to refresh your memory before you continue into this chapter. Though some of the information is reviewed herein, some of the prerequisite information is not repeated.

As you know, child, from our first set of lessons, the tuning is a time of growth that comes to a node in the grid of the universal mesh. The label, tuning, is appropriate to this time of growth because the growth happens when the frequency and tone of the planet, and all things that are a part of that planet, are adjusted into a harmonic agreement with the total of the universal song.

A tuning is required because many unexpected energies of foreign entities have come to this node from their own frequency sick nodes and have altered the frequency of this intersection. As you are aware, child, in the case of earth, the tuning is being done with the help of a workforce who are laboring to tune many individual energies in order to sort out the harmony that will create the resonance necessary for this intersection to be in agreement with the whole mesh.

You are also aware, child, that in a linear sense, this time of tuning will happen in the future. It will only happen at a time when the balance of the magnetic field that holds the matter of the physical earth in place, and the balance between positive and negative, both come to nil point at the exact same time. When this happens, the force of energy that holds the form of physical matter will be released. The form which it takes, once it again takes physical form, will be that which best suits the frequency consensus — positive or negative — of the prevailing energy when nil point is resolved. You are here to be part of the workforce that will provide the positive consensus.

These are all facts you should know if you have understood our first lesson on the tuning. If they seem foreign to you, please review the lesson, The Tuning, from our first set of lessons.

Let us go on with our new understanding to re-examine the tuning. First, let us talk about the timing of the tuning. When will it happen? We know from our previous lesson that it will not happen until magnetic nil is achieved globally and the balance of positive and negative are equal at the same exact time. The physical way this will happen has been explored sufficiently at this point in our first lesson. The nonphysical aspects bear some exploration.

The exact moment of the tuning is unknown. It is unknown to those living in spirit form because we do not live in linear time. All times are now for us. For us, the tuning is today, the very second you read this line of print. It was the very second you read the first line of print in this book. Indeed, child, for us, it happened the very second you drew your first breath, or your mother drew her first breath. It happened the very day the earth took physical shape. Yes, it is true, that living in now means that a spirit (or person who has mastered now) can know the future, for the future is also now.

Yet, the character of frequencies and tones change so quickly on such a place as the earth, where there are countless frequencies causing a cacophony of clashing destinies, that by the time a future date for the agreement of such cacophony is announced, it has already changed formation, and thus changed the linear future. Freewill of the dreamers and the wild fluctuation of the confusion of frequencies in their control makes it pointless to predict an exact time, linearly speaking. For in the time it takes the words to be spoken, the linear time line has changed. In all probability, it will have changed several times before you finish reading this paragraph. This may be a good enough reason, yet it is not the only reason why the exact moment of the tuning is unknown. The exact moment is not known because the moment of the tuning cannot happen until the workforce is ready for it.

We can be assured of this fact by simply looking at our own existence. You exist, child. You must if you are reading these words. Therefore, we know that in "now" beyond the illusion, the tuning of the earth happened and it was positive in nature. If it were not, as explored in our first lesson, Creation itself would not exist. The fact that anything in the dream exists, indeed, that anything at all exists, is proof that the tuning of the earth did not happen until such a time as the positive workforce was ready to create a positive tuning. When that workforce will be ready is up to each and every one of you.

Do not be fooled into thinking you must be a majority in order to be able to tune the planet. You do not have to be more than a handful, in fact. And you are far more than a handful. The truth is, child, the tuning is not like an election. Not everyone gets one vote on how it will turn out. Indeed, child, many people do not have a vote at all. This is not because they are being denied a vote. It is because they do not wish to have a vote. Those who walk among you who have no spiritual direction; those who live only for their physical and creature comforts; those who are lost in the depths of the frequency sick dream, have no vote. Nor do they wish one.

The ones who have the votes are those who are aware of what is possible. Those who understand universal energy and the true nature of things have a vote. Those who are working to create a positive reality have a vote. Those who use this understanding to control and hurt others, even if they are not aware that they are using this understanding to do so, have a vote as well. Those who have a passion for life and radiate their frequency to manipulate that life, for the good or for the bad, have a vote. In general, you could say the greater the passion, the greater the vote. The greater the understanding, the greater the vote. The greater the connection to the universal energy, the greater the vote.

Thus, we can see that is it not an even distribution system. This is a good thing because it means that the more you work on your spiritual growth and awareness, the stronger your vote will count when the planet is tuned. Indeed, as a dynamic soul being, it is your purpose to be a deciding factor in the shape the new tuned earth will take. In truth, child, it is dynamic beings like yourself that will tune the planet.

You may wonder why static beings are not going to be working to tune the planet. There are two strong factors that make the static soul being not suitable to tune the planet. The first is by the nature of the construction of static soul beings, the energy-to-physical link, or what we now know can be called the energy sheathe, is made up of their own energy. If they exert force of intent on their energy sheathes for change, they will affect only their own energy pattern. The static soul being is connected to physicality, or in other words, the earth, by virtue of their coming directly into physical form. Another way of looking at it that you may find easier, child, is that a static soul being's spiritual energy, or energy sheathe, is invested in the physical aspects of the earth. Since the tuning is an energy event, the static soul being's investment is not useful in the tuning.

This is not to say that static soul beings are not useful to the earth or to Creation. They are extremely useful. Without static soul beings there would be no natural sentience to be a living part of the physical node. By their very design, they are a natural part of the physical node. In fact, child, the tuning is all about making the physical node correct for the sake of the static soul beings and their planet. But static soul beings do not have the proper toolset to make the change themselves.

The second reason why static soul beings are not going to be working to tune the planet is simply because they do not know it needs to be tuned. Yes, many static soul beings know that the earth is in terrible shape. Many static soul beings believe things need to change. Some will even work to physically change the world in their own way. They might recycle, plant a tree or two, and even give to animal rights organizations. Nevertheless, the things they do are limited to what their soul type is created to understand. By that I mean, they search for strictly physical options to the world's problems. If they were to hear about the tuning of the earth, it is very likely they would think it was balderdash. That is, if they listened long enough to even form an opinion. This is only natural and expected.

Keep in mind that static soul beings are here to be physically part of the physical clockwork of the planet earth. This purpose is not affected by frequency sickness, although the way they pursue this purpose so obviously is. This is a very different function from that of dynamic soul beings whom are here with a spiritual goal.

Lastly, we know that static soul beings are not going to tune the planet because by their very nature and design, static soul beings' own central frequency discord matches that of the earth. Because of this match to the earth tone discord, static soul beings have no reference to base a tuned tone on.

Let us look at the other side of the issue, child. How do we know that dynamic soul beings are the working force that is going to tune the planet? There are several clear indicators.

The first is that the energy sheathe of the dynamic soul being is made from earth's own energy. This is important. It gives dynamic soul beings some control over that part of the earth energy they possess. And since we know all energy is eternal, when the time of the tuning comes, the full and total of earth's energy will be under the direction of the dynamic soul beings that hold it. That is, each of the dynamic soul beings whose own energy sheathes are strong and stable.

The tuning is an energy event, for as you know, the structure of the physical matter of the illusion will be released at the moment of the tuning in order to be repainted into a new and balanced form. Dynamic soul beings are connected to the energy, since it is the earth energy that makes up their energy sheathes that connects them to the physical. Thus, they have the proper tools to do the work.

The second point we can see that confirms that dynamic soul beings are going to be the ones who will bring on and complete the tuning of the earth node is the fact that dynamic soul beings who are on spiritual mission — or if you will, child, dynamic soul beings who are part of the tuning workforce — must have a whole or nearly whole energy sheathe, or they would not be aware of their spiritual side. Since the dynamic soul beings' energy sheathes resonate to the frequency of the true universal tone, every dynamic soul being whose energy sheathe is whole is carrying with them, on a deep soul level, the tuning fork that will be used to reset the planet's central tone.

The last reason why we know dynamic soul beings are going to be the ones who will bring about the tuning of this node is based on the repeating expression that occurs throughout the physical universe where earth resides. Some dynamic soul beings cause the spread of frequency sickness from node to node. Other dynamic soul beings cure it.

You may find yourself wondering, if you are part of the workforce who will tune the planet, how do you know which tone and frequency are the right ones. Do you need to know what the earth's tone was before the world was corrupted? Do you have to invent a tone that you might think is good for the earth based on your limited knowledge of her workings? Do not worry. It will all fall into place. As you know, the earth's frequency must be fixed into total agreement with the universal frequency in order to be in tune. This means that even though this frequency is well off kilter now, its point of agreement is fixed and will automatically set to the proper frequency when it is attained. This is a good thing, child, for as you know, dynamic soul beings cannot match the universal frequency exactly. As for tone, your energy sheathe is your tuning fork.

Why, you may wonder, child, would Creation design a system where nodes must get sick and need to be cured? It seems rather pointless until you realize two important facts; dynamic soul beings cannot match the universal frequency of the Creation Force, only the universal tone; a node in the mesh cannot match the tone of the Creation Force, it can only match the frequency and find harmony to the tone. This is important because this means that when dynamic soul beings tune a world, they draw the tone up towards the pure central tone. As they do, the higher, purer tone will naturally draw the frequency of the node along with it to match that of the universal song. Frequency is more fluid than tone and changes quicker than tone. Thus, a node will find total agreement with the central frequency of Creation well before it matches the central tone the dynamic soul beings are pulling it towards. Once the frequency matches, the node will come to rest on the next tone of harmonic agreement it reaches and will be in tune. Accordingly, all static soul beings on the earth will be tuned as well, since it is in their nature to match the planet they reside on in both tone and frequency.

It is important to know, child, that the harmonic tone the earth will come to rest on will be a tone that is closer to the true universal tone than it was before it became tainted. Remember this. It is the true reason for tunings in any place, in any physicality. When a node tunes, it grows closer to the Creation Force, just as you do when you tune your energy sheathe and the other frequencies around you. And just like in your life, dear one, it is the friction of the discord in the life of a node that challenges the node to grow.

The node tuning will all happen in less than a nanosecond of physical time, as it will happen in true *now*. When it is over, the earth node will be very different from what it is today. Every source of negative frequency will either be transformed or removed from the node. Cities, power plants, televisions, hatred, evil, and all manner of frequency sickness, and its symptoms will be erased from the earth reality. And it will not be missed. Many souls who had come to the earth simply to be a part of the tuning process will move on after the job is done. This does not mean they will die. Indeed, they will not. For in the moment the matter of the earth is reconstructed, the souls who do not wish to remain on her will intend themselves released to the fullness of the bosom of Creation's love and they will instantly be there. There will be no physical containers left behind, as the matter that makes up their bodies would be adjusted to something else, such as new forest and jungles.

The static soul beings who choose to remain on the planet will suddenly be aware of their spiritual side and their place in the balance of the earth mechanism and the universal song. Everyone, static or dynamic in nature, will clearly understand what you are struggling to comprehend each day on the earth as it is today. Every physical body of every one, including the physical body of the Mother Earth herself, will be whole, complete, and healthy. The balance will be true. The song of the universe will sing in the voice of every chirp of a bird and giggle of a child. All will be pure and in balance. That is, until the next wave of frequency sickness comes to this earth. For frequency corruption, followed by a time of tuning, is the way nodes in the physical universal mesh grow towards total harmonic agreement with the pure Creation Force.

But, let us not dwell on the fact that a linear future holds anything but joy for planet earth and her people. Today, in linear time, you child, stand on the threshold of a wondrous chapter in the unfolding of the prophecy of earth, and indeed, the prophecy of

Creation itself. It is a future that cannot happen without you.

As you can see, as a dynamic soul being you have a great responsibility to keep your energy sheathe as healthy as possible and to be the best you can be with your spiritual goals and work. Your energy sheathe is more than the key to your spiritual health and happiness. It is the most important tool you have. Not only does it connect your spiritual intent to the earth's energy, it is the tuning fork for the planet.

Lesson 10

Physical Frequencies

Up until now, when we have spoken about frequency, we have been referring to your central frequency as it relates to the universal frequency. Universal frequency, as you know, child, is the rhythm of the universal song. It is the frequency of the Creation Force. But it is not the only frequency you will have to deal with in order to work on yourself and your mission. There are literally hundreds of frequencies and tones you encounter every day. You will encounter thousands in a week and perhaps millions in a year. Some of these frequencies will be suited to your personal wellbeing and growth, some will not. When a frequency or tone is suited to your wellbeing and growth, it is said to be in harmonic agreement with you, or that it resonates with you. When it does not suit you, it is said to be in disagreement to you, or it clashes with you.

It is all of these lesser frequencies and tones that surround you every day that you must find a way to bring into harmony in order to be able to shift your central frequency back into harmonic agreement with the universal song. Indeed child, the tones you are exposed to, with time, will directly affect your oh-so important energy sheathe. Frequencies will have an effect on everything else. Physical things are based on frequencies that are derived from tones. Understand, child, that when you read about frequencies in the following lessons, the aim is to address those frequencies that are in place around you in your earth-life, rather than the greater frequency of your central soul, unless otherwise stated directly as such. Also, keep in mind that frequency is the number of times a tone waveform repeats itself, so tone is always a consideration when talking about frequency.

As you know, child, the balancing of frequencies is a must to your health and wellbeing. It is the balance of frequencies that is the key to all cures and all wellness; physical, mental, spiritual, and emotional.

It sounds simple, but it is not. Child, every day you are surrounded by countless frequencies. Some can be considered, more or less, neutral. The rest are either positive or negative in nature. Often, the positive and negative are hard to sort out because it is common practice for negative frequencies to be disguised as something positive to your senses. For example, consider artificial sweeteners. The frequency of the energy that makes up an artificial sweetener is, for lack of a more direct term, artificial. The frequency of the energy that makes up artificial sweeteners is also very bad for your body to absorb. They are not only, admittedly, nonnutritive, they are non-eatable. Yet, to the human body, they taste sweet and rewarding. And to the human mind, they are understood as being good for you because they are not fattening. This is one example where something of foul frequency is presented to, and understood by the general public as being a good thing. I am sure with only a few moments of thought, you can think of so many more. Regrettably, most of the worse frequency offenders are things your paradigm — as written by your society — has convinced you that you cannot live without. Let us explore some of these sources of frequency sickness you encounter regularly.

Unless you live a hermit's life, every day you come in contact with people; family, friends, co-workers, clients, passersby, and other people. As you have probably already discovered through your own experiences, some people suffer such frequency sickness that you merely have to walk into the same room with them to feel the discord. Many people may not seem to affect you that much when you pass them by, but their negative frequency does brush your own frequency. If you encounter this same type of personal frequency over a prolonged time, even if it is casual in nature, it will begin to affect you. It is fortunate, child, that the same can be said for your interactions with positive people.

Frequency conflict or not, you must interact with people. When you run into people who are projecting a lot of negative energy, even if it is not directed straight at you, be mindful that you do not absorb it. Take a moment to envision yourself surrounded by a pure positive frequency energy space. Do not think of this pure energy so much as a shield, but more like a personal positive frequency area that will dissolve any negative frequency that comes near it. Do not be afraid to ask a spirit guide or teacher, or even the universal Creation itself, to help you create this space.

If you expect to run into a person of poor frequency, envision this surrounding energy before they even get near to you. You may find that if you do, their negative attitude will not cross the barrier, and by the time they reach you, they will be far more pleasant to interact with.

If you find you encounter a lot of negative frequency driven people each day, you may even want to make a mental connection to your vision of surrounding energy and an object, such as a pendent or ring. Associate the object with the instant creation of your positive frequency area. Use the object to remind you of your positive frequency space so you can create it quickly when it might be needed. You never have to close your space, thus recreating it just makes it stronger.

Although other people with deep frequency sickness are a bother, child, it is not the negative people that do the most damage to your energy sheathe and surrounding frequencies. Most of the damage inflicted on your energy sheathe and on all your other frequencies is done by way of your television and radio.

Televisions themselves, as machines, give off foul frequency. This is particularly true for those with large cathode ray tubes. For a cathode ray is a negatively charged particle of energy. But the damage done to your frequency by television is far more than that. The programs on the television, particularly primetime programming on major networks, are so chock full of negative frequencies that to sit and watch one hour of television is like living several days with a negative person.

Many of you, child, will find this statement to seem like nonsense. After all, you say, you watch your favorite TV show and feel great after. This may be the case, since I cannot answer to what each and every one of my readers watch from day to day. I cannot state indisputably that the television show any one of you watched at any time was a carrier of frequency discord, but odds are good it was. For I must say, if you are watching any entertainment television show produced since the early 1980's and believe you are not being exposed to foul frequencies, you are fooling yourself.

The early 1980's were a time of great change for the people of the earth. Without going into any discussions about political and social ramifications of the time, it was a time when the dynamic soul beings on the earth came to know in their higher beings that the tuning of the earth was certainly going to happen. If you were alive during this time period, your higher soul being was part of this decision. Once it was realized that the tuning was imminent, many spirits that were to join the workforce on the earth at this time made their appearance on the physical world. Thus, the early 1980's saw the first true wave of what you call indigo children. Though I feel I must point out that the spirits who came in these waves of children are not stronger or better than the ones already here or the ones yet to come. It was only their arriving in such numbers, in such concentrated areas of the world, that caused them to stand out anymore than the previous spirits who took to human form.

As we mentioned before, the influx of spirits to physical form on the earth piqued the interest of beings whose intentions were not in the interest of a positive tuning. Thus, it was about this time that these beings, if you will, kicked their work into high gear. Their work was insidiously sly. These sly beings of malicious intentions approached mankind in his weakest spots — his greed and his want for technology. Thus, it was not long before the poison, high fructose corn syrup, was widely introduced into the diet of people around the world. High fructose corn syrup is the root of many human aliments, including type 2 diabetes and some forms of bipolar disorder, as well as certain forms of asthma. On a physical, scientific level, this can be easily studied and verified. Nevertheless, since physical science is limited to the illusion it is part of, it fails to see the frequency reason why high fructose corn syrup is so bad for you. That is, as you may guess, it is bad because it has an artificial frequency that is extremely harmful to the frequency of your body. High fructose corn syrup is only one of many unsuitable, uneatable, and frequency sick substances that have been added to the food supply.

You may believe that there are scientists and agencies working for you to be sure your food additives are safe. This is the case, at least on the surface. But with the frequency sickness inherent in the system of all governments, and with greed being a great motivational tool for industry, the good of the people can be compromised. Because of this, child, many of the things people ingest each day are adversely affecting their frequency.

You may be wondering what could be worse for you than ingesting frequency sick foods. Yet, the frequencies of the additives in your food chain are easily rivaled by what you ingest with your eyes and your ears every time you sit in front of your television.

You see, child, it was about this same time that the makers of television shows were inspired to discover that they could apply audio and visual

145

frequencies to their television shows to manipulate the reactions of their viewers, in much the same way makers of commercials had been using embedded images for more than a decade earlier to control peoples' responses to their products. From the early 1980's onward, you will find more and more television shows infused with both audio and visual frequencies designed to do everything from make you love a certain character and hate another, to desire the type of soda the character is holding or the type of car he is driving. On the surface, this may seem harmless enough. Yet, child, it is not the intent of the unnatural frequency, it is the frequency itself that does harm to you. That is not to say that the intent of all frequency interference in television shows is harmless. The powers that be have included frequencies in programs with the intent of making a population docile, have them accept wars, promote nationalism, and encourage them to hate a particular ethnic group.

I realize, child, this all sounds a bit "over the top", but it is not a conspiracy theory or paranoid fantasy. Even if you could remove all the embedded frequencies purposely put into your television shows, you could, at any moment of the day or night, find on your television a channel broadcasting the most polluted of frequencies. The visions of horror that humans regard as entertainment is abhorrent to their spirit guides and teachers. Movies and shows abound that do such things as glorify war, take your imagination into the mind of a killer, show graphic scenes of murder and assault, depict sexual crimes, show people behaving horridly as they try to destroy each other on reality shows, listen to people argue and yell at each other, or wash their soul's pain like so much dirty laundry on talk shows, and the list goes on and on. Even shows that are meant to make you laugh, are often based on the symptoms of frequency sickness, as if it is normal that all people should behave so poorly.

If you, child, think spirits too prudish, think again. It is not a tendency to be straitlaced that causes us to disapprove of human entertainment. It is because we can see what it does to you as a people, and you as an individual. This is not to say, child, that you can never turn on your television again. I know that would be too much to ask from some of you, child. Nevertheless, I will go so far as to ask you to give more thought to what you choose for entertainment and be sure to do something positive to balance the negative influence of your television time.

The same can be said for the radio. Some songs are uplifting, some are not. The frequency of sound is a strong motivator. You know what music sounds good to you, and what does not. There are many songs with both positive and negative hidden frequencies. Just as with artwork, which also can have positive or negative frequencies in it. Often the artist is not even aware what frequency they intend the work to carry. The work simply reflects their soul's balance at the time the work was created.

Be cautious of music that has a melody you enjoy but a negative message in the lyrics. The fact that you enjoy the music will encourage you to open up to it, and without knowing it, you may absorb the negative intentions of the lyrics.

Be particularly mindful of talk radio shows. Listening to talk radio shows for long periods of time, especially when you are sleepy or when you are doing something that demands a certain amount of concentration, such as driving, has a semi-hypnotic effect on the brain. The more you listen to a person talk when you are doing something like driving, the more your state of concentration causes you to absorb what is being said, as if you are being brainwashed by the speaker. Indeed, on some level you are. As you absorb the opinions of the speaker on your radio, any frequency discord that speaker projects becomes a part of your inner song, and will have a real effect on your body.

As you know, child, from our first look at the physical body and how it is affected by frequency in book one, there are many other things that can harm your frequency, and thus cause you physical harm.

Thankfully, there are ways you can adjust frequency to help bring your body up to where it needs to be frequency wise. It is important to understand that because you live on a world that is out of tune, and your body is made up of the substance from that world, and even your energy sheathe is created from the energy from that world that is not tuned, no dynamic soul being will ever be totally and completely tuned until the earth is also tuned. This does not mean that you cannot get as close as you can. But it does mean that you will always have to work to maintain your frequency in the proper range, particularly when your physical body is subjected to great sources of discord.

The tuning of the static soul being's body is a bit easier than the tuning of the dynamic soul being's body. A static soul being's body, as you know, is connected to the earth on the quantum energy level with energy from that static soul's own higher being. Because of this, when a static soul being is out of frequency alignment with his or her body, the being's energy body goes out of alignment to the same degree. When you adjust the frequency of a static soul being's soul energy, the body he or she resides in will automatically follow suit. Thus, to bring up the frequency of the mind is to cure the body.

It is a bit different for a dynamic soul being. When a dynamic soul being first falls out of frequency alignment, his or her body and soul may or may not start out at the same point of discord. Because the energy that connects the dynamic soul to the physical is not made up of the dynamic soul being's own energy, it will not automatically draw up the physical frequency when energy frequencies are lifted. Thus, over time, dynamic soul beings will find they go in and out of harmonic agreement with their own bodies.

When dynamic soul beings work on frequency clearing and adjustment, they may bring their soul into harmonic agreement with their body and many of the physical symptoms of frequency sickness will go away. But in time, if they do not keep their soul frequency in adjustment, or if they raise their soul frequency up without working to raise the frequency of their body up with it, they will fall out of harmonic agreement and the symptoms will return. In a case where the soul frequency moves up and out of agreement with the body, the body must be adjusted up as well in order for symptoms to stop. This is often overlooked. When it is, the dynamic soul being may have a relatively clear frequency in the astral body and energy sheathe layers, but have a very sick physical body and aura. Indeed, many do.

How many people do you know who work very hard in their spiritual life only to be sick all the time with chronic illnesses such as allergies, headaches, digestive problems, reoccurring infections, and other such ailments. This is because these people do not understand the nature of their own being. They do not know that they have a dynamically structured soul, and therefore, child, they do not know that they must work on the frequency of their physical body separately.

Lesson 11

Adjusting Frequency to Heal the Body and Mind

Child, the tools of healing are all around you, just as the tools of harm are all around you as well. Before you begin to use the tools of healing, you must first do your best to remove that which is harmful from your life. Letting go of some of these things will be difficult for you. Some may be impractical for you. Nevertheless, child, the quicker and more thoroughly you remove these things from your life, the faster you will be able to fix your frequency and heal your body.

I am sure you have heard much of what I am going to say from other teachers before me. Some of you, child, may have already made these changes. Some of you may believe you cannot make these changes because of circumstances in your life, or because you do not believe they will make a big difference when compared to the effort you must expend on them. However, without making at least some or these changes in your life, you will have a much harder time balancing your frequency.

In order to remove as much of the foul frequency as possible that you are exposed to every day, you must do the follow things.

You must avoid your television as much as possible. Even a reduction of an hour of television time can make a difference in your life. When you do watch television, do your best to make better choices. Avoid viewing television shows full of disturbing images for your entertainment. If you watch the news and see disturbing images and hear about disturbing things, take a moment to focus on those things turning to the positive. Allow the images to motivate you to create and share healing energy with those affected by the situation.

Drink water. Drink at least one to two liters a day. Drink real "living" water. By that I mean spring water. Do not drink distilled water or reverse osmosis water. This is important. The water you drink must be living water. When water is distilled or put through a reverse osmosis filter, all the minerals, and thus, all the frequencies in the water are removed. Water was created to carry frequencies in the minerals. And that is what it does best. Water that is created by way of distillation or reverse osmosis, at best, has no frequency. So it does you no real good to drink it. It may quench your physical thirst, but it does nothing for frequency thirst of the body. Indeed, some people who only drink such frequency-bereft water will develop eating disorders, as their mind confuses the need for water frequency consumption with the need for food.

Water is a natural conductor. It is one of the best conductors for life frequency. When distilled or reverse osmosis water is left sitting for any length of time, it will actually draw in the frequency of what is around it in order to fill the void. Often, this means that if you purchase your distilled water at the store, your water is not only void of any good frequency, but it is full of the negative frequency it has picked up along the way, such as what was given off by the trucks it was transported in, and even of the hurried people who rush past it while it sits on the shelf in the grocery store.

If you use a reverse osmosis water filter and drink your water directly as it is dispensed into your glass, you may still be drinking negative energy, for reverse osmosis filters work slowly, and thus keep a reserve of water in a tank from which you drink. This reserve tank is often stored near electrical components. So, in the end, you are ingesting the frequency of the machine itself.

Regardless, if the water picks up unwanted frequency or is frequency dead, when you drink distilled or reverse osmosis water, you are not doing anything for your frequency health.

Resolve to drink living water. Choose spring water, or if you have a good well source, you can choose this. Never drink chemically treated water, such as what comes from most taps. Since water carries the frequencies of what it is exposed to unless it is filtered naturally by the earth, tap water, even if processed through the best water treatment facility, will still carry some of the frequencies of the impurities and sludge it once held. This is in addition to the frequencies of the chemicals used to clean it, and any additives put into it.

Another thing you must do your best to remove yourself from is automobile congestion. I realize eliminating the use of an automobile would be almost impossible for many, child. Automobiles have become such a necessary part of your life. This is why

I limit this suggestion to avoiding automobile congestion, or traffic, rather than suggesting you do not use a car at all. Of course, if you could live your life without using a car, that would be best, but it is not practical in the confines of the world in which you live, child. Nevertheless, if you must drive, do your best not to drive at times when you are bound to be stuck in traffic. The amount of foul air given off by automobiles is only rivaled by the amount of foul frequency they emit. It is no wonder that road rage is becoming so common in cities where people must face such frequency discord daily. Avoiding concentrations of automobiles and the drivers under the frequency stress those automobiles create will do much to help your frequency.

Avoid food additives. Especially avoid such things as high fructose corn syrup — which is also known as glucose fructose syrup — nitrosamines such as sodium nitrite, artificial sweeteners, monosodium glutamate, artificial colors and flavoring, etc. In general, it is better to eat single ingredient foods when you can. If your food has an ingredient that comes from a laboratory rather than a natural source, know that it will not be beneficial to your frequency.

Especially avoid any foods that have been genetically altered. Since natural foods are not frequency sick to start with, if you change the DNA artificially, you create an unwholesome frequency in an otherwise wholesome food.

Avoid eating meats, especially meats from animals given growth hormones, steroids, antibiotics, or other chemicals. If you must eat meats occasionally, avoid eating the meat from animals that feed on frequency sick food.

If you drink milk, drink organic milk. This is especially true for women and girls.

Do not over medicate yourself. If you need a medication to help you until the time that your frequency is such that your body heals itself, then the benefit may outweigh the harm, and thus this becomes a necessary evil. But do not rely on medications for your health. Never take medications you do not need. Particularly avoid serotonin uptake reinhibitors. These medications have an effect that is extremely damaging to your energy sheathe. They stifle your creative energy and dull your psychic senses. They should only be considered in life or death situations, while other means are put in place. They should be stopped as soon as possible. Something as simple as adding real licorice, and perhaps some ginseng to your diet, may allow the natural frequencies of these herbs to help with depression.

In truth, the only real cure for depression is to adjust the poor frequencies that are causing it. Serotonin uptake reinhibitors suppress frequencies, and this is why they will often stop depression. But they do not cure it. They simply dull the ability to feel frequencies, so the one who takes it does not feel the strong frequency discord that is causing the depression. If the root of the frequency disruption is not addressed, the problem will grow until the medication can no longer stifle the awareness of it. When this level is reached, the person will believe that their depression has returned worse than ever before. But in truth, the root problem never went away at all.

Another unfortunate effect of these medications is that they dull all good frequencies as well, and this stops personal growth.

This said, it is understood that there may be some of you, child, who have frequency discord that causes physical and emotional illness that these, or perhaps other types of medications are needed for. Even if your condition is considered chronic, try to realize that as you work on correcting your frequencies, your body will heal. Once the particular frequency or frequencies that are at the root of your condition are corrected, you will be able to stop the medications. Indeed, child, as you work on healing yourself, you may find that your medications will start to cause unwanted symptoms if you stay on your usual dose. For example, if you are taking medications to regulate your blood sugars, you may find that if you remain on the same dose, your blood sugars will drop too low. If these things start happening to you, it would be wise advice to visit with your doctor and speak together about lowering your medications until such a time as you can remove them from your life entirely. Do not stop taking necessary medications until you have spoken to your doctor and are sure you have healed to the point of no longer needing them. I know some of you, child, may wish to throw your medications away at the first sign of improvement. But you must adjust your body, not shock it. Your body is accustomed to the frequency created by the medications you take. The more medication you take, the more discord the medication is either causing, masking, or both. Unless you have mastered the concepts of now and of the Creation of the physical, you cannot expect your body to become totally tuned in an instant. Just like it takes time and many sessions of tuning to bring back the tune of an old piano left out of tune for years, most of you can expect that it will take time for you to bring your body to the point where your medically necessary medications can be stopped. Yet, with persistence, it will happen. Indeed, some of you will have results very quickly.

The last thing I would like to list that you should avoid in order to help you adjust your frequencies is the company of people who can do nothing but gossip viciously about other people, or complain about how hard life is. No one really likes to be around people who complain about everything, are never happy, and have not one kind word to say about anyone else. Yet, it seems everyone encounters such a person in his or her life at one time or another. Some of you will have such a co-worker. Some might have a relative like this. Some might have such a neighbor. Aside from being tedious to endure, such people are accurately described as being walking frequency germs. When they complain and gossip, what they are really doing is passing on their negative frequency to those around them. Every word such a person speaks is filled with frequency discord that wants to attach itself to you in the same way a sneeze would be filled with germs to make you sick if the person had the flu.

You would not sit there and let someone with the flu sneeze on you repeatedly, would you? You would find a way to politely excuse yourself, then you would probably wash any places the sneezes wet you with germs. Yet, so many dynamic soul beings, by virtue of their empathic nature, believe it is their obligation to sit quietly and absorb the germs of negative frequency from such people, regardless of how uncomfortable they feel, when they know they should politely excuse themselves, then take a moment to clean off any negative frequencies directed to them.

Keep this in mind the next time you run into such a person, and take the proper precautions you need to in order to avoid letting them spread their frequency discord to you. It is also good to note that when you do this, after a while, the frequency germ carrier will see that it is pointless to try to infect you and will either stop or move on to another victim. This will greatly help your frequency.

As you can imagine, child, there are many more things you can do to stop hurting your own frequency, so you can begin to heal. Think of other things on your own. Do your best to keep positive frequency in mind so you can heal your frequency.

Healing your frequency is an important thing you must do in order to make yourself feel better. The fascinating thing is, since physical life is an illusion, you can change anything, including your frequency and your health, simply by "knowing" it is fixed. Unfortunately, because you are immersed in the illusion, few, if any of you, child, can do something so directly to affect the illusion. Most, if not all of you, child, will benefit from the use of tools to help your frequency to adjust.

The first tool you have all around you every day is the plants and trees of nature. Though the Mother Earth herself is not in total balance, natural things are far more in tune than manmade things. Even if you live in the busiest city, or you are housebound, you can find objects of natural frequency wherever you are. A single leaf from a tree holds the frequency of the whole tree in it. You do not have to have a tree in your yard. You can pick up a leaf at the park and take it home to have the energy of a tree with you.

If you are housebound, you can do the following frequency healing technique with a houseplant. You do not even have to have a plant in your home, though plants are good for everyone to have in their homes. If you have no tree or plant around you, look for some other natural thing. If you cannot find anything untouched by the technology of man in your home directly, look in your refrigerator. Do you have a head of lettuce, a fresh raw carrot, or an uncooked potato? These things will suit you just fine when nothing else is available.

The first step, child, is to sit where you can see the object of your focus. If you are indoors, take your natural object in hand and sit comfortably by an open window in natural daylight. Bring yourself into a meditative state, then focus your energies on the natural object. Explore it with your eyes and with your fingers. Feel it with all your senses. Especially project your psychic senses to feel the object. Sooner or later you will begin to feel a pleasant, calm energy from the object. In general, the bigger the object, the quicker you will feel the energy. But the size of the object does nothing to change the energy. It only affects how quickly the energy will build. Tree energy is tree energy in a forest or in a single leaf. It is likely you will feel tree energy quicker if you sit in a forest than if you sit in your parlor with a leaf in your hand. Nevertheless, once felt, the power will be identical.

When you have found the special energy of your chosen object, focus on that energy growing around you. Visualize in your mind's eye the energy as a soft cloud covering your body. Imagine the energy cloud as pure air. Take deep, deep breaths, and breathe in that air. Breathe in the energy. Relax and allow the frequency of this energy to fill you and help adjust your frequency. Do this every day. If possible, do it two or three times a day. You do not have to use the same object each time. You can use any tree, leaf, or carrot. You can use anything natural at all.

For example, if you are away on a business trip to a city where concrete has replaced every tree, you can still do this, even if you can only find one single blade of grass growing in a sidewalk crack. Indeed, child, there are no excuses not to do this simple exercise. Even if you never have occasion to step outside, if you can save one piece of celery or one leaf of lettuce from your lunch, you can do this. There is no excuse for not helping yourself with this simple exercise. It is a powerful tool. The more you do it, and the more variety of natural objects you choose to do it with, the greater and faster you will see marked improvements in your frequency.

Another simple exercise anyone can take part in includes acknowledging and thanking the spiritual energy in food. It does not matter what you are eating. It does not even matter how natural a food you are eating. Be mindful of the energy you are consuming. Be grateful that it is there for you.

This brings to mind, child, something to help your frequency that is extremely important for you to remember. Regularly take the time to acknowledge that there are many people who have souls just as real and as valued as your own who are starving every day. There are many people who are the innocent victims of frequency sick nations and armies who are murdered without mercy each and every day. There are those who live in conditions so abhorrent to you, child, that you would not wish to see a rat living in such a way. Compassion for these people is one of the greatest gifts you can give yourself, and one of the strongest tools for overall frequency adjustment.

I am sure you have heard it said, child, and you may even believe the schools of teaching that tell us that these people are in such terrible situations because they are repaying a debt of karma they incurred in a past life, or the law or attraction drew the souls to that place. Both of these explanations are lacking substance. For as you know from our first set of lessons, child, when one dies and leaves this dream, one is reunited with Creation and understands all. The spirit becomes aware of mistakes and what was learned from such mistakes. One would feel no need to punish oneself by making one destined to physically suffer. And as for the law of attraction, in some sense it may have played a role, as it may have attracted one soul to come into the illusion with another whom it is connected to, and thus attracted to. But, all told, it is not a soul's inner frequency pre-set to suffering that causes that soul to embody itself in such situations. The law of attraction does not work that way. In fact, the law of attraction is so misunderstood by many of the people who know of its existence that they believe it is a magical money machine.

The reason for the existence of the starving sufferers is not as important to this lesson as it is for you to understand, child, that we are all united as one energy. When you see suffering, famine, disease, and other forms of strife, you must try to understand that you are suffering along with those people. What can you do, child? After all, if it were in your ability to stop world hunger you certainly would, I am sure. But in truth, it is in your power, child. It is in the united power of all children of light.

More than sending money or clothing, more than giving your time and efforts, which are all good things you should do if you can, you should take time each day to focus on a better world for these poor souls. Visualize the hungry fed, the suffering comforted, and the world at peace. When you see anything negative in the world, create a vision in your mind of it as it should be. If enough of you, child, were to visualize the destitute as being housed, fed, and happy, then believe it or not, reality would change and in no time at all things would be such that these poor souls were housed, fed, and happy. And since we are all one, when these people's frequency is better, so will yours be.

Remember, thought is God. Concentrated, focused thought, especially when shared among great numbers of people, forms a consensus. With a consensus of enough individual thinkers who understand that their thought is powerful, all agreeing on a reality, that reality will manifest itself. It must, because with unified understanding and consensus, it becomes the will of God.

Compassion for the poor is one of the greatest gifts you can give yourself. This is because as the poor are comforted, the consciousness of mankind is a little bit better. As the consciousness of mankind heals, so shall the earth. Your compassion, even if you never touch one person physically, will bring some comfort to those who suffer, by way of the spirit realms, where the high, pure frequency of compassion travels best. Your compassionate prayers will return to the world in the form of spiritual peace that will make a difference, not just for the poor souls, but also for yourself. For when you project such high frequencies into the world, they will return to you, amplified. This, too, will raise your frequency.

Thus, when you see the troubled people of the world, realize that there is a need for your focus of compassion, and give it without measure. This is the very least you can do. If you can do more, do that as well.

Let us look at another way each of you, child, can help yourself. Do you recall, child, that water is a natural holder of frequency. This makes water a wonderful tool for bringing the correct frequencies into your physical body. As I mentioned earlier, you should be drinking between one and two full liters of living, tuned water a day. Do you know that you can tune your water by adding frequencies to the water before you drink it? The process is a simple one, but to do it correctly, you must do a bit of homework. Before you add a particular frequency, you must know what the frequency is.

There are two basic methods for putting frequency into water. In order to produce the clearest, longest lasting infusion of frequency into water, it is not enough to just tell your water what frequency you want, you must first know what the frequency you want feels like.

Let us use the example of sunlight. You know what it feels like to stand in the sun on a beautiful day. In order to charge your water with sunlight, imagine that sensation until it feels very real to you. Then, using your psychic energy and will of mind, put your hands in or around the water you intend to give the frequency to, and project that feeling into the water. After a moment, stop and take a few breaths, then put your hands to the water again. This time, rather than pushing the feeling towards the water, sense the feeling of the energy coming from the water. It should feel different than it did before, at least on an energy level. You may even find that it physically feels different as well. It should feel like sunlight to you, at least on a psychic level. If it does not, then start again until it does.

As you can imagine, it can take some time to infuse water with a large variety of frequencies. Nevertheless, the infusing of frequencies one at a time, and with active intent, is the best way to "charge" water. Everyone can charge water in this fashion, though few take the time to.

The second basic method often used to charge water is done with a more general frequency. Rather than thinking of individual frequencies, you can think of what you wish the water to do. For example, you may wish your water to cure a cold. So to that end, you would project into the water the idea that the water will be a cure for a cold, and let the universal forces figure out what frequencies need to be in the water. Those who do this must have a strong trust in the universal forces. Through this trust, the activation of energy will occur that will put those frequencies into the water. If the trust in the universal forces is not so strong, the charging of the water might not be very successful. It is wholly dependent on the energy control and ability to project intent of the individual who is charging the water.

If you intend to charge a lot of water at one time, rather than charging it daily, be mindful where you store your charged water. Once charged, water will not remain pure to the charge it is given for long if it is exposed to other strong frequencies. It will also naturally lose any charge given to it over time regardless of where it is stored. How long a charge will last depends on the strength of the intent put into the water and the location of the water with respect to any other strong frequencies. Positively, wonderfully, charged water can lose its charge quickly if exposed to strong sources of negative frequency or strong electromagnetic fields. Keep this in mind.

The charging of water is not a new idea. Mankind has been charging water for centuries. In fact, child, the origin of baptism has it roots in the concept of working with charged water. In the case of baptism, it is the emersion of the body into charged water.

Everyone has the ability to charge water with general frequencies as well as individual ones. Some people have a natural ability, or worked their abilities to a greater level through practice to be very strong. For, like most things, the correct charging of water takes practice. Water charged by a person who has mastered the art of infusing water with frequency can be very powerful indeed.

Some of the people who are very good at charging water with frequencies will make their charged water available to those who are not as adept, and those who do not wish to go through the bother of charging their own water, as well as those whom need very powerfully charged water right away and believe they do not have the time to learn how to charge their own water to such powerful levels. So long as you know the water you get has been charged correctly, and it has not lost its frequency from storage over time, or by bombardment with clashing frequencies, there is nothing wrong with using water charged by another.

Nevertheless, working up the skills to charge water to carry the precise frequencies you wish is beneficial and not difficult. It just takes time. With practice, you can add frequency to your water. Indeed, water is such a frequency magnet, once you get started, it can be hard not to add too many frequencies to your water. It may sound rather strange, dear one, but you should never express anger or hatred near water you intend to drink. For, indeed, the water could easily imprint with such poor frequencies.

It has been suggested that if you know how to use dousing rods or a pendulum, you can use such devices to check the charge of your water. The method is clearly subjective, but some have used it with great success. If it is something you are interested in trying, here is how you would proceed. With rods, you would start by standing by your uncharged water. Walk away until the rods cross or open, as the case may be. Then charge your water. Use the rods again and see how much further you can go before the rods react. With a pendulum, hold it over the water before and after the charging and see if there is a difference in the movement of the weight. Better yet, have someone who does not know what you are doing test your water before and after. If you can enlist the help of someone who does not believe in charged water or dousing, ask him or her to walk with the rods or hold the pendulum. This way you can have a degree of impartial verification.

When choosing what frequencies you should charge into your water to help correct frequency sickness, you should individually add to your daily drinking water the frequencies of as many beneficial herbs, plants, trees, sunlight, minerals, amino acids, and other good things of the earth. You should add the power of positive energy, the four directions, primary colors (red, yellow, blue), as well as love, hope, and joy. You should also add the power of universal truth, peace, serenity, balance, and compassion. The frequency of all good things and all good emotions should be infused into your water one by one. If you are not feeling physically well, be sure to add the frequency of healing and recovery.

Of course, most of you, child, will not have the time needed to add each frequency individually. In such a case, you could strongly intend that all these frequencies come into the water without thinking about them and infusing them individually. But this is not as powerful, in general, as doing them one by one. A good compromise would be to infuse each day's drinking water with this general frequency intention, then take a moment to reinforce particular frequencies by infusing them individually. Sunlight, primary colors, and the pure tone of the musical notes "C", "E", and "G", are some of the more important to overall frequency balance, particularly for dynamic soul beings. Indeed, if you have little time, be sure to at the very least, take the time after you charge your water in a general way, to charge your water with the individual focus on sunlight, the primary colors — which hold all other colors in harmony, and form white light — and the pure tone musical chord of C major — as expressed with the notes of C, E and G — which is an audio frequency match to primary colors that hold all other colors, and thus, the chord of C major holds all other sound frequencies in harmony.

Water is more than the fluid of life, it is the fluid of frequency. By charging your water with good, high frequencies, you create a beverage of life. Drink it freely and you will soon find the frequencies it contains will become part of your body and soul. It is a must to frequency healing.

You may argue, child, that you do not like to drink plain water. This is a symptom of frequency sickness. The fact that you find the perfect fluid for your body, indeed the only fluid your body was designed to use for hydration, as something disagreeable, is clear evidence that you truly need to drink frequency charged water. If your water is charged correctly, you are likely to find that it tastes better than water straight from the bottle. If this change in taste is not enough to encourage you to drink, or you have a hard time bringing yourself to drink as much as needed, try infusing the water with the energy of something natural you enjoy drinking, such as fruit juice. You may be pleasantly surprised to find that water infused with the frequency of orange juice will present a hint of orange flavor on the tongue. If you cannot drink one to two full liters in a day, do your best to drink what you can, and you will find that as the water adjusts your frequency, it will be easier and easier to drink your liters and you will come to truly enjoy it.

In addition, if you live in an environment that is harmful to your health, consider moving out of the area if this is feasible. Do not choose a home near high tension power lines or a substation. Do not buy a house downwind from a factory. Do not rent an apartment in a downtown area where the air is full of automobile exhaust. If at all possible, do not take a job working with plastic resins, or harmful chemicals, and so on.

If you are a static soul being, this is just about all you need to do to keep yourself in a state of relatively balanced tuning, and stay healthy. Yet, if you are a dynamic soul being, you have one more issue. As you do all these things and raise the frequency of your soul, since it will not automatically pull the body up with it, you will need to do a few more things that will help adjust your body along with your soul energy.

As you know, child, by their nature, dynamic soul beings have a strong central tone, but a central frequency that is easily adjusted. Because of this, the lesser frequencies, which are apart from the central frequency of the dynamic soul being, are much more sensitive to frequency discord. As you may be aware, child, you are far more emotionally sensitive than most others around you. Your feelings are easily affected by the feelings of others. Even those of you, child, who have developed a hard façade, know that this is true. Indeed, it is this overreaction to the emotions of others that leads you, dear one, to build such a façade in the first place.

Dynamic soul beings surely will find life a struggle when they are surrounded by unsettled energies. The passions of others' emotions are something a dynamic soul being must learn to deal with on an emotional level, otherwise their own inner feelings are condemned to be as fickle as the wind, forever changing with the whims of those around them, and they will build inner walls of defense.

How often, as a dynamic soul being, do you find yourself, child, becoming the reluctant receptacle for another person's emotional baggage? How often have you found yourself in a situation with a person you barely know, if you are acquainted at all, imposing upon you his or her life's story in great detail? How often has your whole day been ruined by a momentary brush with a belligerent individual?

It is the same for all dynamic soul beings. This is why so many of you, child, have learned to build walls around your inner selves. These walls are intended to protect you. It is unfortunate that walls not only function to keep unwanted things out, but they also function to keep things in. These emotional blocks dynamic soul beings carry inside, behind the protective walls, are the root of many a physical and emotional illness. For this reason, the first step each and every dynamic soul being must take in order to heal and become strong is to tear down the walls.

This does not mean that you must leave yourself unprotected from the effects of others' pain. It means that you must learn to develop new tools for processing these unwanted, uninvited emotions so you can allow your own to come through. It is not a difficult thing to do. The hardest part about learning this new method for dealing with other people's uninvited emotions is to break the habit of believing you have some responsibility for emotional frequencies that are not your own. This is not to say that you should never give sympathy or comfort to someone in need. Far from it. Sympathy, compassion, and comfort are all very important gifts that when shared in a balanced and healthy way, do wonders for your frequency health and that of the person you share with. Never turn away a person in true need of your compassion and sympathies. Giving of your compassion, love, and sympathy is unquestionably one of the greatest things you can do on this planet. Yet, you must understand the difference between giving of your compassion and love, and allowing others to give you the responsibility for their emotional state. It is important to always give of your heart, your understanding, your compassion, your love, and your sympathy to people, but do your best to avoid absorbing that which belongs to them and should be — and indeed, must be — processed by them.

There are many more people you will meet who will project a need for your help but, child, the need they project is not truly genuine. It is an unfortunate truth, but a truth regardless, that because of their frequency sickness, many people will not process the issues and emotions they should in order to be healthy. Rather, they prefer to delegate their personal responsibility for these issues to anyone willing to absorb them away from them. It does not matter to them which receptacle they choose for their pain; a friend, relative, or stranger on a bus. It only matters that they can unload their emotional frequency baggage on someone else's shoulders with the hope of freeing themselves from the struggle it creates in their soul. Far too often, it is dynamic soul beings they seek out; for experience has taught them, on a deeply subconscious level, how to seek out and identify such beings. Far too often still, the dynamic soul beings engaged by such people, by virtue of their easily adjusted central frequency, will, without much forethought, and regardless of how uncomfortable the situation makes them, dutifully absorb the offending discord from the intruder. This leaves the intruder feeling relieved and settled, but leaves the dynamic soul being shaken and disturbed. This, in turn, encourages the dynamic soul being to build inner walls for protection from any future invasions.

Since, as mentioned before, inner walls are also barriers, there are better ways to deal with people who wish to unburden their frequency issues onto your shoulders. The first and most important step is to become aware when this is happening to you. Far too often, child, you do not know that you are being used as an emotional bandage until the event is over. You must make the effort to be aware of when another person is using you as his or her emotional sponge. This is particularly important if the person you are being abused by has a habit of using you so poorly. Once you are able to recognize when you are being used, rather than building a wall to separate yourself from the energy and frequency being thrown at you, make the conscious effort to say to yourself, "I am not responsible for this person's issues." Know this.

Since thought is God, if you start to imagine feeling as they do, you will create that frequency in your being. You must not internalize the other's feelings upon yourself.

Remember that having sympathy is to have an understanding and a regard for what someone else is feeling. It is not the act of internalizing the other's feelings as your own. The internalization of another's feelings is empathy. Empathy, for the most part, is a greatly misunderstood ability that is rooted in the universal song, and is another issue we will talk about at another time.

If you do not allow yourself to internalize other people's emotional issues, they cannot force you to take those issues and the frequency discord that comes with them. When dynamic soul beings internalize other beings frequency issues, their own frequency is affected. Since the issues are not truly their own, the dynamic soul beings have no tools, or even a frame of reference, in which to work out such issues and heal the frequency. The unfortunate result of this is that the dynamic soul being will become physically ill as they battle the frequency. Or, worse, their subconscious may even take action to recreate the other person's issue that they internalized in their own lives, with the hope of finding a way to resolve the issue. As you can imagine, this can be extremely unpleasant.

The most important thing to do when you encounter such as person, after you realize that you are being used, is to stop the interaction. This is easy if the person is a stranger on a bus. If you feel uncomfortable, simply say, "Excuse me, but I feel uncomfortable knowing such personal things about a stranger," and turn away. The person may think you rude, but do not worry. It was truly rude of him or her to attempt to use you to begin with.

If you do wish to talk to this person, or the person is a friend, or someone else close to you, keep conscious awareness in your mind that you are not responsible to absorb the frequency discord the person is offering you. Sympathy demands you consider how they feel. It does not demand that you *feel* how they feel. Remember this. It is an important distinction. As a matter of fact, if you begin to feel as a person feels, you cannot feel the compassion you should feel for a person in pain. When you block out your feelings of compassion, you deny both you, and the person you work with, one of the highest healing forces.

If you find that you have empathized incorrectly with an individual and you are carrying an emotional burden that is not your own, you must take steps as soon as possible to clear yourself of the emotional burden. The longer it remains with you, the more accustomed you will become to its discord, and the more it will harm you.

Meditation is the strongest tool for isolating any discord that is not your own and releasing it. Here is a simple narrative to help you understand the use of meditation to clear yourself after such encounters.

In our example, Ann is a dynamic soul being who has just talked to her best friend, Pam. Both Ann and Pam are married. Pam has recently had an emotionally heated argument with her husband. She phoned Ann and told her all about it. Ann, without realizing it, for she is so close to Pam that Pam's energy is common to her, has internalized Pam's frequency discord in the form of emotional stress. When Ann hangs up the phone, she is feeling odd, even sad.

Ann realizes that she has absorbed Pam's frequency and quickly resolves to use meditation to remove the offending frequency from her own. Finding a quiet spot, Ann meditates in her usual manner. For Ann, this includes candlelight and a small relaxing water fountain, gently gurgling by the window. Once she is relaxed, she focuses on isolating the feelings she experienced after talking with Pam. She identifies each in turn, labeling it as best she can. She is not worried that she will not get them all, or she will get too many. She knows that does not matter. She imagines she is holding a bouquet of brightly colored balloons. She chooses colors that make her happy. Then, as she identifies each feeling, she imagines attaching that feeling to the string of one of the balloons. She does this for each feeling she identifies until her bouquet of balloons is full of feelings on the strings. Then, with a heartfelt and heart-made intent of healing, Ann envisions her hand releasing the balloons. She watches silently as they float away, higher and higher into the sky. She does not wonder where they go. She knows that they will end up where they belong. Meditation over, Ann regains her physical awareness without Pam's frequency baggage.

If Ann had waited a while before trying her meditation, it may have been harder for her to know the difference between her own emotional frequencies and those of her friend's. If she had waited even a few days, it may have been impossible for her to distinguish between the two. For by then, Ann's soul would have accepted the discord as her own. In such a case, Ann might have even found herself picking a fight with her own husband, not realizing that by doing so, her subconscious was making an attempt at creating a point of reference, or source for the feelings it does not have one for at present.

Indeed, child, Ann's meditation was a powerful tool. You may be wondering how something as simple as the visualizing of balloons could be considered powerful. The answer is interesting. Visualization is a tool that helps people focus their thoughts. Although it is surely true that all people are energy beings and have the ability to change anything in the illusion with just their thought to change it, few of you, child, are so understanding of the dream that you can operate beyond its limits without tools.

Visualization is one of the strongest tools you have. Imagination is a key to many things. I am sure you have heard it said, if you can dream it, you can be it. This is true. At least it is true within the confines of the mindset of those that dream it. We will talk about this in more detail in our next lesson. For now, know that visualization, particularly visualization during meditation, is a powerful tool that allows you to do things you may not be able to do otherwise.

When we look at the example of Ann and her balloons, we can see what she really did, if you wish to be technically exact, was to isolate interloping frequencies, group them together in a cohesive form, then by the power of her will, adjust them to neutral tones whose resonance pattern no longer interfered with her own physical frequency patterns and that of the central frequency she is adjusted to. This sounds a bit more complicated and a bit harder to put into effective practice than simply visualizing the tying of feelings on balloon strings and letting them go. Through the act of visualization, she was able to do a very complicated series of frequency adjusting functions, simply and effectively.

Remember the balloon meditation, child. It is useful for many minor frequency issues. You can use it, as in the example, when you have accidentally internalized someone else's frequency discord. It is also very useful when you want to release anxieties, frustrations, anger, and the like.

By avoiding the internalizing of others' emotional frequency discord, and by meditating to remove anything accidentally absorbed, dynamic soul beings will come to understand that they do not need to keep an inner wall and will naturally take it down. Taking down this wall is an important step in drawing up the body to match the higher frequency of the soul.

Another thing that is of paramount importance to the tuning of the dynamic soul being's body to match the frequency of the mind is the addition of higher dimensional frequencies to their body.

Since dynamic soul beings are naturally from the spirit world, the frequencies of the spirit world are strong in their soul. When a dynamic soul tunes during frequency healing, he or she naturally draws to energy of the nonphysical type natural to him or her. Since the dynamic soul being's energy sheathe is not made up of his or her own soul energy, the energy sheathe will naturally tune to a more earth-based higher frequency, taking the astral, aura, and physical with it. When this happens, the body and the soul will no longer be in harmony and the body will experience the return of previously healed symptoms.

In order to avoid this, or to reverse it if it has already occurred, dynamic soul beings must accustom their bodies to the housing of higher spiritual, nonphysical frequencies.

The first thing you should be doing in order to help your body make this connection is contemplate, meditate, and absorb yourself daily in the energy of the higher place where you come from. Of course, child, this can be tricky to do if you do not know or understand what you are looking for; and indeed, the central soul frequency of such energy will be different for every individual dynamic soul being. So, in this case, rather than focusing on connecting to the frequency of the higher self, you should be focusing on connecting to the universal tone of the higher self. After all, child, all dynamic soul beings share a common central tone. With so many, indeed, an infinite number of dynamic souls in existence, all singing the same unified tone, this tone is powerful indeed. As you know, the tone remains the same regardless of the frequency. Even in music we see this. A pure C note is a C note if it is played at the frequency of middle C or at the frequency of C above high C. A C note is a C note regardless if it is played in a high or low frequency. The central tone of the dynamic soul being is the universal tone, regardless of the frequency it presents itself at.

So, child, understanding this, we can see that dynamic soul beings are all single notes in different scales, so to speak; and by focusing on the tone of this single note becoming one with the physical body in a comfortable frequency, the dynamic soul being can use this tone to adjust the body. This is done by way of meditation on the tone.

To find the tone, you can use visualization to see the tone as white light. You may even be able to find an object or tool that represents the tone you associate with your inner song. Many of you, child, find the tone in music. Some will find it by way of singing bowls. Some of you will never actually need to hear a tone to understand what it is. For indeed, child, your central tone is not a sound at all. It is not a color at all. These are creations of the dream. Your central tone is the breath of God. It is the feeling of the Creation Force alive in you. It is something that is beyond the physical. It is that part of you that sometimes makes you feel like all you have to do is raise your arms into the air and you will ascend to the sky. Capture that feeling and you will come to understand the universal tone.

Once you have even the smallest inkling of what the universal tone is, focus on it, nurture it, contemplate it, and meditate on it. But most of all, visualize it as becoming one with your physical body. Let it enter your physical body and infuse itself into your very cell structure. With each breath you take, visualize you are breathing in the beautiful tone. Fill your mind with it until your body is filled as well. Do this often. The more you do this, the quicker your body will become accustomed to the new energy pattern and the faster your frequency sickness will heal.

Another way of bringing the universal tone into the cellular structure of your body is to add it to the charged water you drink daily. For all dynamic soul beings, it is of the utmost importance to add the central tone of existence to water charged for consumption. Indeed, child, though it may seem unusual, you should be mindful to add this tone to the very waters you bathe or swim in, not just what you drink. It is of greatest healing and enlightening powers, and is indeed the root of the act of baptism. For, child, baptism is far older a custom than any religion that lays claim to it, and in its original form, it was seen not only as an act of purifying with blessed water, but also of healing with it.

When adding the universal tone to your water, be sure to always add it as an individual item. Do not use generalization methods to infuse this most important energy into your water. Put your all your heart and intentions into imprinting your water with this energy. By doing so, you are sure to give your water the strongest healing abilities you can.

Drink freely of your universal tone water and it will infuse the physical/energy connection that holds your soul and physical body in synchronization with the proper "quantum glue", if you will, child, and your body will come up with your soul. If you have left your body behind, it will soon catch up with you and you will be whole and well again.

Once you are whole and healed, do not become a slacker. Until you are living on a totally tuned planet that is free from any discord, your soul and your body will be subject to the influences of poor frequency. You must, at the very least, maintain your work on your frequency purity and tonal agreement. Even better, child, you should consistently be reaching for more. For once your body is in check, and you know how to keep it in line with your soul growth, you are free to reach for as must spiritual energy, enlightenment, and conscious awareness of the universal order as you wish.

Lesson 12
Manipulating the Illusion

There are many things you can do once you understand frequency sickness and you are aware of how to adjust your frequency in order to correct your situation. Let us talk about the adjustment of frequency sickness and the ways you can make these adjustments for yourself and for the planet.

The first thing you must understand is that no one on earth will ever have a perfect frequency until the earth is tuned. For as long as the Mother Earth is experiencing frequency discord of her own, none whom exist on her can hope to find a perfect balance. This does not mean that you cannot come close to a perfect balance, and indeed you must come close to a perfect balance in order to move forward and tune the planet so that all will be in balance. But how?

Think back to the beginning of this book. Lesson 1 says, "You are thought. Thought is energy in a pattern. The pattern that energy takes is thought. Thought is you." We also learned from lesson 1 that God is thought. Now, think back to lesson 5. It says, "All energy has, and indeed is, a vibrational frequency pattern." Thus, child, we know that since you and God are thought, and thought is energy, it follows, given that energy is a vibrational frequency pattern, that you, child, and indeed the God Force itself, is truly only a pattern of frequency. And it goes to reason, child, that since the God Force is eternal, as you yourself are, that you and Creation are the total of ALL vibrational frequency patterns.

Nothing around you, not one rock, not one cell of your body, not one drop of water is anything but energy in a certain form. All things physical, everything you can see, touch, and taste is a pattern given to a frequency of energy vibration. Everything, absolutely everything in the illusion and the greater dream, is simply thought. This is without exception.

Whose thought? The thought of God, of course, but also, your thought. You are the thinker. All around you is your eternal thought. Thus, everything around you made from that thought, which is everything, is under your control. You can think it as you want it. It is that simple and that difficult at the same time. You are one with the Creator of thought. You are that thought. You are the thinker, or in this state, the dreamer. It is up to you to find the power to control your thoughts and to apply those thoughts as you need to.

Keeping this in mind, child, we discover that frequency sickness is simply the physical and mental manifestations of the wrong kinds of thoughts. It is almost like a self-feeding machine. Your frequency discord encourages you to think disharmonious thoughts, and your disharmonious thoughts cause frequency discord. But there are things you can do to break this cycle.

In our first book of lessons we talked in detail about magnetism and how it affects matter and the tuning. To refresh your memory, magnetism is the force that holds matter in physical form. It has three positions or manifestations, positive, negative, and nil. It is at nil that the illusion of physical reality is free to be rewritten globally. That is, provided that the balance of positive and negative forces at play on the earth are in balance at the same time. As you know, which ever force is in control when the nil point is crossed will be the authors of the form the new earth will take.

Did you know, child, that aside from global tuning of the node, your body can be tuned in much the same way. Of the several methods for helping your body and soul come into proper tuning, the one that uses nil point thought is, by far, the most unlikely method you will use. Nevertheless, it is the most direct of all ways to affect the material configuration of the illusion, not just for your body, but for all things around your body.

In brief, nil point thought is a method that creates both a limited magnetic energy nil, as well as a balance between positive and negative, which allows small sections of the illusion to be reorganized, or rewritten, instantaneously. Understanding nil point thought is important to understanding the working of the physical universe, even if not everyone will be able to harness the power of nil point thought. With this in mind, let us take a look at it.

You, child, are a complete being. This means outside the dream, and the illusion, you are all energies positive and negative. Yet in the dream, and indeed, in the greater illusion, you are not complete in your focus. Your positive energy focus and influence should be dominant over any negative aspects of your being. This means over all, that your frequencies should be of a higher focus the majority of the time during your physical life. Because of this natural focus on the positive, many people who are trying to grow spiritually, mistakenly work hard to forget that there is more to an eternal being.

Child, you may be fully aware that you are an eternal being, but do you limit your views of that eternity which you are to only what you perceive as good? Do you ever look at and embrace the whole of who you are, not just the angelic, but also the evil? You may be wondering what point is there in giving any focus to the negative side of eternity. After all, giving it focus will only strengthen it. And in most cases, child, you are correct to wonder, for in most cases, to focus on evil is to strengthen it. Nevertheless, if you are exploring the nil point method of bringing your body into tune, you must look at the total of eternity as far as you can comprehend it, without a filter to remove the darker side of the preverbal coin.

The key to this type of body tuning and manipulation of physical matter is your ability to find the nil point in the balance between the positive and negative aspects of your soul. Contemplate this point and do your best to be aware of it. It is the point inside of you where there is no good, no bad, no positive, no negative. It is the point where everything you know, do, say, and most importantly, think, has no identity. It is the place where thoughts are completely neutral. It is a difficult place to find. Nil of the mind is a place much sought after by gurus, monks, and other holy men through the ages. It is often describe by such seekers as a total emptying of the mind, having no thoughts at all. But it is truly not an emptying of the mind. It is the point of nil in the mind where every positive and every negative perfectly balances and cancels out each other, leaving only the perfection of nil. The emptying of ones mind is not as powerful as the nil point of thought. To empty one's mind is to be out of touch with your own God Force power. To be in nil point thought is to perfectly balance all aspects of self into one point of total agreement. In order to achieve nil, you must work on understanding the truth of your eternal state of being. That is, your true eternal being, not simply your linearly eternal state of being. You must recognize and work to balance all positive and negative thought. You may find this easier to do if you visualize all of eternity being folded in the center point (if such a thing were possible) and know in your heart that the center point you created is that place in all of eternity where all things balance out, leaving no positive or negative. This point is nil. Once nil is achieved, you are in total harmonic agreement with the universal song. You are one with Creation, and the Creation Force that you are becomes active. And, just as with the overall tuning of the earth, when nil point is achieved globally, the thought that takes control after the nil is broken is what will come into physical being. In other words, once you are at nil, you are free to tune your body and even change that which is physical around you. This is done in the following way.

Before you start, be clear on what you wish to achieve, or what you are going to tune first. You can choose to change your entire being at one time, or make something manifest in your hand. For the sake of example, I will pick one aspect of the body someone might like to work on, such as a minor health problem. For instance, let us assume the problem you would like to work on is a damaged knee. Rather than focusing on the idea of healing your knee, visualize yourself, as strongly as you can, walking without knee pain. Visualize until you are feeling as if you could get up at that moment and walk without pain. Memorize the feeling of this visualization in such a way that you can call it to mind quickly and surely.

Next, achieve nil, as described above. Do not be discouraged if you cannot achieve nil when you first try. It is an exceedingly difficult thing to do. With much practice, everyone is capable of achieving the nil state of mind, although few, child, put sufficient time and effort to the task to achieve it. Nevertheless, once nil is achieved, hold the focus for as long as you can. The longer you can hold nil, the stronger the force will be when you break nil. When you first achieve nil, it is likely the length of time you can hold the state will be measured in seconds or even half seconds, so do not be discouraged if the state seems to be fleeting. When you feel you are ready to let go of the nil point, or as you feel it is about to slip away, quickly call to mind your positive focus that you have committed to memory. For example, see without a doubt that you are walking with a strong normal knee. When nil resolves itself, it will bring into reality that which you envision. When you are once again in the illusion, that which is around you will be changed. You will have used the nil point to rewrite your own personal reality.

It sounds quite simple, and indeed it is, provided you can successfully achieve true nil, which is far harder a task than you may imagine. For most of you, child, this method of rewriting the reality around you, though achievable, will prove to be too difficult a task to pursue, if only because your position in life makes it impossible for you to devote the energy it takes to be successful. It is not because you are not adept or strong enough, it is simply because achieving nil requires a massive paradigm shift in the way you perceive reality. This shift is extremely difficult to make for those who are living in the depth of the illusion. The tremendous effort it takes to make this shift is the reason why holy men of many religious orders are often solitary in nature. They believe that through their solitary lifestyle, away from the distractions of life, they will be free to find the key to nil point thinking. Nevertheless, few ever achieve it.

Those who can make this shift and achieve nil point thought will find that they can change the illusion in many ways, not just in their physical health. People who can achieve nil can learn to use it to manifest physical matter from pure energy. They can also use this great ability to change the physical reality of those they interact with. They can do what you would call miracles.

It is unfortunate that not many of you, child, will achieve nil point thought. Indeed, if enough of you learned to apply nil point thought to the Mother Earth and her inhabitants, the world would be tuned already.

Luckily, for those of you, child, who find nil point thinking allusive, there are other ways to rewrite your reality and bring actual physical change to your life. You will learn to change the illusion around you through work on frequency agreement in order to remove your personal frequency sickness and move on to tune the planet of her frequency sickness.

With a heavy heart I say, it is regrettable that the earth is not in tune, because this means that there will always be some kind of frequency discord around you that you will have to deal with. Even if you moved to a primitive village with no electricity in the middle of the most remote place on the globe, you would still be exposed to some amount of frequency discord. As you know, child, frequency sickness is a global affliction. There will always be frequency sickness until the Mother Earth herself is tuned.

This can be seen when you think about the illnesses that animals suffer. The majority of animals on this planet have not been tampered with by any off world interlopers, yet they all suffer illnesses. Animals in the deepest rainforest are still subject to diseases from time to time. This is because the Mother Earth herself is so off frequency that the very animals that are in tuned with the original song of the planet are, by way of the earth's corruption, no longer in harmonic agreement with the planet. In other words, when the earth went out of tune, the animals that lived on her that were once in tune with her found themselves suddenly out of harmony.

Therefore, it stands to reason, that no matter how properly tuned your body becomes, you will still be subject to some of the earth's defenses. The closer to a universally pure tone you maintain and the better you maintain your frequency harmony, the less likely you are to become sick, and the quicker you should heal, but it does not mean that you will never be sick again so long as the Earth herself is sick. Nevertheless, child, if you know how to change your reality through manipulation of physical frequencies, you will know how to correct the circumstances of your life, and the world around you.

Let us look at the most common and easy way you will be able to manifest changes in the illusion. This is by way of the energy of high agreement, or what you may commonly know of as the law of attraction. Put simply, it is the method of adjusting thought to bring about real change in your life.

The law of attraction as portrayed today is actually a misunderstanding of a basic agreement in the connection of a person and his or her higher self. It is not a law at all. It is often described as a force of nature that draws to a person the object of his or her thoughts, so long as that person focuses on the object. Within a limited scope, this could appear to be true. Nevertheless, it does not accurately represent the mechanism of high agreement. Indeed, child, such an explanation only focuses on one small aspect of the phenomenon as it relates to one section of the population. By limiting high agreement to the attainment of physical wants, you limit a wonderful tool of growth to something quite cold and cruel.

The energy force of manifestation through high agreement was never designed to be the money making machine it has been ascribed to be for the last hundred years or more. This is particularly true for dynamic soul beings. And indeed, child, when the dynamic soul beings who are aware of spiritual goals try to use it as a way to become physically wealthy, it will often backfire on them with opposite results.

Let us explore what this energy really is and what it is not, so that you can use it correctly. The popular premise is based on the truth that like attracts like. Thus, the premise goes, like thought will attract like things. Therefore, if you focus all your energy on wealth, beauty, or a new sports car, you will become rich, beautiful, or get the sports car of your dreams. These things will be "attracted" to you because the frequency of your thought will force the universe to manifest these frequencies in physical form for you. The premise states that it is a force as strong and as constant as gravity. The premise goes as far as to say that it works like an indiscriminate magic wand that when commanded by thought must give you exactly what you think about, good or bad. Luckily, for everyone in physical form, this is not a correct representation.

It is sad, indeed, that the true and complete nature of the law of attraction is not known. In truth, the effects of the nature of high agreement that is mislabeled as the law of attraction is not a physically based law, such as gravity. It is not a law at all.

In brief, the energy force of manifestation — or high agreement — is the method of reaching an agreement with that part of you which resides beyond the physical illusion in order to adjust the frequencies found in the active laws around you that will, in turn, change the greater reality around you. And, as you may have pondered, child, it works differently for static soul beings and dynamic soul beings.

Before we go too far into what high agreement is and how you can use it, let us exam the nature of the two types of laws that affect that which happens on physical worlds. The first type of law that governs things in physical existence could be called set laws. These are things that are considered to be physical truths in physical existence. Gravity is one such set law. It is something that happens to all things evenly.

What goes up must come down. It happens without anyone having to think about it. No one makes any decisions that cause the thing that went up to come down. This is an example of a set physical law. Since the entire physical structure of the illusion agrees to these laws, they are slow to change frequency patterns and thus harder to overcome from the dreaming state.

The second type of law could be considered active physical laws. These are things that are more easily affected by frequency. An example of this type of law would be inertia. Inertia is a name given to the concept that a physical object in motion will continue to move until some other force pushes upon it to stop it or change its direction. Since energy is in motion in the case of active laws, they are more subject to frequency influences.

It is true; thought is the God Force. So, when enough energy is given to thought, physicality can change. But it is also true that there is more to your thought than what you are thinking in your physical body at this moment. Remember child, you are an eternal being and your thoughts are not limited to that which is housed in your body. This is the root of high agreement.

High agreement, as the name implies, occurs when the wants, thoughts, and wishes of the embodied part of your soul — that part of you that has physical awareness — comes into total agreement with the total of your higher self outside the illusion. It is simply your higher self reaching into the illusion, at your request, in order to give you the tools you need to do what you are designed to do. Yes, child, that is all it is. And it is wonderful.

When you focus your thoughts on changing the things around you, your thoughts are so powerful that you can do it. That is, if the thoughts of your higher self are in agreement with what your earthly self wants. The particulars of how and why high agreement creates manifestations or why it fails to work, as you might have ventured to guess, differs for static soul beings and dynamic soul beings on a planet that is out of tune.

First, let us look at the overall method for working with the energy force of manifestation and creating high agreement. The first thing you need to do in order to make a change in physical reality is to visualize what you want. You must make the visualization very firm in your mind. Then you must come to know in your heart and soul that you are going to have what it is you visualized. You must know it so strongly that you will have no doubts about it coming to you. Frequent meditation on what you want will enhance your ability to make it come to you. Then, you wait and it will be there. In theory, it will be.

What you are really doing when you visualize something so strongly is focusing the energy of your higher self on creating what you want in your life. If your higher self is in agreement, the combined energy will help to create the method for your getting what you agreed on. Since physical reality is an illusion, your higher self energy, when activated in such a way, will operate from beyond the illusion to bring events into play that will bring you what you want.

The difficulty is that your higher self and your conscious self must be in agreement. Here is where the difference between the static soul being and the dynamic soul being can be found. For by the nature of each, the types of requests their higher selves are apt to agree upon will differ greatly.

Let us look at static soul beings and their relationship to the energy force of manifestation in a frequency sick world. The frequency of the static soul being is more in line with the sick frequency of the planet. Thus, the static soul being is more directly connected to those things on the planet that cause frequency sickness. Or, in other words, static soul beings are drawn more to physical objects than to spiritual goals. In addition, the static soul being's higher self is designed to be focused on physical existence. The focus of that soul's higher self is to be a working physical part of the planet the static soul being lives on. Because of this, when a static soul being invokes the energy force of manifestation by way of his or her focused thoughts to get something of physical pleasure that he or she believes is necessary to his or her being a happy part of planet earth, such as money or a new car, the static soul being's higher self will be prone to agree easily. The static soul being's higher self, whose focus is to direct the part of itself that is incarnate to be in harmony with the planetary tone, is likely to see these objects as being part of what physical life on the planet is about. The desires of the static soul being, when focused on with great passion, as seen through the filter of the planetary discord, may appear to the incarnate part of the being as a very important need, and thus the static soul being's higher self will want to do what it can to provide such a needed object. Therefore, in the case of the static soul being, if the focus on physical wealth and other creature comforts is strong enough that he believes he needs them to be necessary to his happiness on earth, the higher self will agree and the power to manifest these things will come.

On the other hand, child, in the unlikely event that a static soul being wanted to manifest something purely spiritual in nature, for example, the ability to understand universal order, it is not likely the static soul being's higher self would agree. After all, the understanding of such things would be contrary to the prime need of being a physical part of the physical workings of the world.

For a dynamic soul being the energy force of manifestation works a bit differently. Since the higher self of the dynamic soul being, by its nature is spirit based and not focused on being a cog in the workings of any planet, when a dynamic soul being requests anything of a physical nature using the energy of high agreement, his or her higher self will only agree if the physical need is connected to the greater good of the spiritual nature of the dynamic being.

For example, if a dynamic being were to focus on having a new sports car, yet there was no spiritually related reason for having a new sports car other than because the dynamic soul being wants to impress his friends, there would be no agreement with the higher self and it would not manifest, regardless of how hard his physical awareness focused. Indeed, child, if a dynamic soul being focuses too much of his or her physical awareness on the having of material wealth that has no direct connection to any spiritual considerations, the higher self may even feel compelled to give the physical self a wakeup or shakeup of sorts, and work to actively block such things. Thus, it is not uncommon for dynamic soul beings who try to use the energy force of manifestation to garner wealth and property to find their efforts backfiring until they get back on the correct spiritually focused path.

On the other hand, when a dynamic soul being focuses his or her thoughts on the manifestation of spiritual energy, awareness, growth, and spiritual prosperity, these things are sure to come in abundance. In fact, child, for a dynamic soul being, the way to find true self-reliance, monetary security, and other creature comforts is through the results of spiritual growth. For as you spiritually grow, you become a more important part of this earth game on the side of universal growth, and the universe will reward you with all you need.

One function of the energy force of manifestation through high agreement that works the same for both static and dynamic soul beings is that of physical healing of the body. It does not matter if you are a static or dynamic soul being in nature, your body is an important part to your reason for being in the illusion at this time. Therefore, your higher self has incentive to agree with your focus to heal yourself.

Visualize, with all your heart and soul, that your body and mind are physically well, and your higher self will help you get there by helping you fix your frequency discords. If you can maintain this visualization long enough, in theory, it is all you need to do. But few of you, child, can keep up such pure visualizations for as long as they are needed to create strong results. So to speed up your healing, in addition to visualizations, do what you can to remove frequency discord from your life and the other things we spoke about in our last lesson, and you will find it will not be long until your physical, emotional, mental, and spiritual wellness are restored to the universe's plan for you.

One more misconception that must be addressed concerning the current misunderstanding of the workings of the law of attraction, or high agreement, is that if you think the wrong thoughts you will attract harm and hurt to you. There is some truth to this. If you obsess with thoughts of illness and pain, you will create these conditions in your life. But the key word in the last statement is "obsess".

Remember, the response to your requests for manifestations comes from your own higher self. Your higher self is not going to strike you with cancer if you spend time with a friend who is suffering with the illness and needs to be comforted. Indeed, by helping your friend, you are creating the two highest frequencies you can from your physical state, love and compassion. You will not be stricken down, but uplifted by sharing your friends concerns. If human beings could easily call illness upon themselves simply by thinking about that illness, there would be no doctors who were not racked with disease before they left medical school.

As you can see, child, the incorrect interpretation of the law of attraction lacks the most important of all social emotions — compassion. For in the popular concept, good or bad that comes to you is attracted by your own thoughts. Thus all victims actually call their fates to them by way of incorrect thinking. Of course, this makes little sense when you apply it to the infant beaten by a frequency sick caretaker. It is simply nonsense, if not pure debauchery, to believe that a child could be responsible for attracting her own beating. Such things are not caused by attraction. Illness, in all its forms — physical, emotional, spiritual, or mental — is caused by frequency discord. It is an unfortunate truth that everyone on a frequency sick world will fall victim from time to time, and in one degree or another, to the symptoms of another person's frequency sickness. To live on a frequency sick planet is to live with discord.

Do not turn your back on the things of this world that require your compassion and attention for fear that thinking about such things will attract those things to you. It does not, and will not, work that way. For in order for something to manifest by use of this force, your higher self must agree it is for your greater good.

Also understand, child, that this does not mean that everything bad that happens to you in your life is because your higher self wishes it for your greater good. Even though it is hard to understand that in the true universal order no mistakes are ever made; in the illusion, in a frequency sick body, on a frequency sick planet, surrounded by other frequency sick individuals whom have freewill, bad things are bound to happen to good people. If it were not so, you would not be here to tune this planet.

Also know, that even with the best intentions, there will be times when you will work perfectly on your end, focusing for the manifestation of something that you feel you need for the proper reasons, and yet it still will not happen. When this occurs, know that you have not failed. Remember, no matter how hard you focus on manifesting a change in the physical earth dream, if your higher self is not in agreement, it will not happen. Also, if what you desire requires voiding the freewill of another, it will not happen; f or your higher self would never agree to take away the freewill of another.

Also, child, if your desire challenges a set law of nature, the effort needed will be much greater than what it would need to be when your desire is based in something rooted in active cause and effect.

It is curious to many of your teachers, dear one, that so many of you become frustrated when faced with certain examples of things you want that directly conflict with the physical laws of nature around you. Yet, you have no problem at all accepting the fact that you cannot change other physical laws of nature.

Consider, you do not think twice why you cannot meditate for a few moments and master the art of levitation. Indeed, child, many of you may even snicker at my even mentioning it. Yet, at the same time, you expect other set physical laws of nature to break simply because you wish them to. Because your physical body is in the illusion, your physical body is subject to the set physical laws of the dream until such a time as you can see beyond those limitations. Until you can believe you are able to levitate, and then simply bypass the physical law of gravity and levitate at will, you cannot and will not be totally free from all of the effects of set physicals laws.

For example, some of you, child, may be frustrated because you cannot lose weight simply by thinking thin. Others may be frustrated because they cannot cure their bloating on a diet rich in lentils and beans. I pick both examples concerning digestion for a reason. What you put into your body is going to be processed by the laws that govern the set physicality of your body. If you continue to eat high calorie foods and do not work to burn them off, you cannot think thin and expect to be thin until you can levitate, for you are fighting the same force. If you eat a diet of flagellant forming foods, you cannot assume to feel no bloating, unless you can fly, for you are defying the same laws.

It is not that correction of these issues is not possible, for all such things can be corrected. Nevertheless, in order to fix such issues with direct thought, you must understand what you are working with first. In order to change any physicality, you must approach it one of two ways; either you supersede the laws of set physical reality (and learn to levitate at will in the process), or you work with the frequencies around you and recreate the dream from within at the quantum level where energy and matter meet in the form of frequency.

Just as with nil point thinking, the direct approach is the one less chosen. Few of you, child, will ever master levitation from your current physical state. Nevertheless, most of you, if not all of you, will become masters of frequency.

Do you recall, child, the instructions for adding frequency to your water in order to adjust your body's health? You can use much the same method, with a little adjustment, to create positive frequencies in your environment. You can also use it to promote positive frequency in your future.

Remember, "now" is all times and "here" is all places. In true reality there is no beginning, middle, or end of anything, including time or space. The place you exist, and the moment you are aware of, are the only place and time that matters. This is a powerful tool. If you can fill "here and now" with positive frequency, you are filling all the moments of your life and every place you will ever be with that same positive frequency. You can reach to that positive frequency for help in times when "here and now" greet you with discord. Remain present in now. Since the future will someday be now, to master now is to master the future.

Always do your best to focus on what you are doing now, how you are feeling now. What you are experiencing now. Let go of the past. Good or bad, the past is no longer important. You have already experienced the past, even if you feel your understanding of it is incomplete. Let go of the future. Good or bad, it will be what it is, based on what you are experiencing now. So as you can see, the best way to have a good future is to have a good now.

When you master here and now thinking, you will find that the things you want will be there when you need them. You will not have to concentrate on manifestating anything you want or need in order for it to become available to you. Because, child, everything you want or need is manifested somewhere right now. And since all places are here, and all times are now, then what you need is right in front of you. It may sound strange, but try it before you doubt. Those who master a life in here and now are not limited by anything physicality can throw at them, not even physicality itself.

You will be truly happy living here and now. For when you live here and now, you do not create the discord worrying about what the future brings with it. You do not hold on to the discord you experienced in the past. You are free to experience the singular joy of the singular moment. With joy comes frequency healing. With frequency healing comes everything else.

Your teachers understand, child, that truly living in the here and now is exceedingly difficult for those in physical form. This is why many tools are given to you in order to help you adjust your frequencies that are not dependent on your ability to live here and now. Tools are a necessary part of the manipulation of the physical, because they allow you to focus that which is nonphysical in nature into a physical form you can understand.

There are many, many layers at which you can perceive actions in physical reality. The most basic of these ways is by scientific cause and effect. You are very aware of this level and have grown so accustomed to it that it is hard for you to see the energy and frequency levels of cause and effect. This is why the embodied find it so important to use tools to do things that are really functions of energy and frequency.

For example, it is customary for many religions and cultures to spiritually purify an area by use of some kind of smoke or incense waved in a censer, or burned in an open container. This custom goes far back to the earliest versions of man. Yet, is it really the power of the smoke or smell of the incense the drives away any unwanted impurities? Is the smell of frankincense or sage so commanding that it prevents evil beings from entering the room? Or is it the frequency created by the consensus of the people who believe it works? Indeed, it is. Child, if you truly believe that a tool will work for you, it will.

Tools are a gift given to you by your teachers to help you overcome your self-doubt. Though it may seem odd to those of us outside the earth illusion, we know that you are more likely to put your total faith in a rock, incense, or other tool than you would put in your own ability to change reality. This is why we give you tools. This is why we impress upon the tools we give you our own energy and the energy of your higher self. Because we know you value tools, we do our best to make them useful for you. Use the tools given to you by higher forces. You will know such things when you find them. Do not be afraid to ask your higher self and spirit guides to empower your tools. Do not forget to empower your own being into your tools. And use your tools freely as you wish.

However, always be mindful that if truth were told, child, there is no tool in all of physical existence that is as powerful as your awareness of here and now and your understanding of your one unity with Creation and the thought of God which you are.

The Earth Game
Revisited

So, now child, your mind is filled with here and now and you are working hard to adjust your frequency. But what about this earth game? What about all the players? What about the rules?

As I stated at the beginning of the lesson about the earth game, that lesson and the next that concerned the players was offered to you for reference. It is interesting information for you to know, so when others approach you with questions about aliens and spirits you will know a little more about those beings than you may have. Yet, the knowledge of the earth game, players, and rules really does not do much more than fill you head with facts that are trivial when compared to the rest of the knowledge base you have gained through our lessons.

It is trivial because it is rooted in an open secret. By that, I mean, the root of the game is no secret at all, but few of the players will ever admit to knowing it, never mind admit to understanding it. This secret is that the game is already played, won, and over. The only players on the field, the only players who were ever true players were you, child, and those like you. Everyone else turned out to be just spectators in the stands. You are the dreamers. The dream is yours. Creation is in your hands. Be good to each other.

Some Common
Questions

Q: If the aliens, spirits, and other beings around the earth are only spectators, then why do they interfere with the game?

A: Because the true players allow them to. Just like in any sports event you might attend on earth, the spectators' cheers and taunts affect those on the field. Likewise, the spectators in the earth game may sometimes become over zealous and run out on the field, so to speak.

Q: I believe I am a dynamic soul being. I believe my partner is not. Is there any hope for our having a spiritual life together?

A: It is extremely rare for beings of different soul types to be attracted to each other long enough to develop such a relationship. For this reason, it is highly unlikely that your partner is not a dynamic soul being. If your partner appears not to have a spiritual interest in life, consider that your partner may have built very strong walls to protect himself or herself from frequency discord. Also consider that you or your partner may have experienced a quick change in your central frequency which created a cacophonous frequency clash.

If you still love your partner and wish to remain with him or her, and your partner feels the same, it would do good for the relationship to find an activity to share that is not heavily rooted in a spiritual nature but has spiritual overtones, in order to help reopen spiritual awareness in your partner. Walking on the beach, hiking in the woods, even bird watching, just about anything that involves nature are good choices. This will help you open up to each other once again.

Be careful not to push your partner to a frequency he or she cannot endure. To do so will force your partner to leave your life by one means or another. But be mindful not to lower your frequency to accommodate your partner. It is sad to realize, but if your partner is steadfast in his or her refusal or inability to come up in frequency, the best you can hope for is a cordial relationship of, perhaps, comfortable friends or child rearing partners with separate spiritual goals.

Q: How long will my water stay charged?

A: The answer will vary depending on the circumstances. It is best to check your water to be sure it is charged correctly each day. You cannot overcharge your water.

Q: Can I charge my orange juice, tomato juice or other beverage?

A: Yes. Anything that contains water can hold a charge, including other beverages, and even foods. But only water holds the strongest, most easily absorbed charge. Do not forgo your water in favor of any other beverage, even if you have charged it.

Q: If I achieve nil point thought, will I be able to perform miracles like curing the sick with a touch of my hand?

A: Yes. If you achieve nil point thought you will be enlightened and empowered in the same way and to the same degree as those who have achieved it before you. Use it as wisely.

Q: Scientists have been working on curing illness by altering the DNA of people who have illness. If they succeed, would it be wrong to allow myself to be cured with such methods?

A: This is a tricky question. If the work done returns DNA to a normal state, then in theory, the answer would be no. It would not be wrong for you to have any abnormalities in your DNA corrected by medical or frequency means. Yet, in its current form, DNA adjustment done by medical means is not truly a correction of an individual's abnormal DNA, so much as it is the attempt to replace an individual's damaged DNA with normal DNA from another source. Since DNA carries with it, on the quantum level, both a physical and psychic connection to the unique individual that DNA belongs to, you will be infusing your body with another individual's central tone and frequency. If the donor and the recipient are of different soul types, the combination could be quite harmful.

Rather than depending on science to cure you, child, work to re-write your reality and cure yourself. After all, if you can repaint a planet, you can repaint anything.

Q: What will it really be like after the tuning of the earth?

A: Wonderful.

Thoughts and Notes

Thoughts and Notes

For more information about
Alex or Michelle Wedel, and to hear or read
more inspiring and informative channeled
messages from Alex and other spirit teachers
please visit:

www.spirittalker.com

For more information please contact:
Sweetgrass Press L.L.C.
P.O. Box 1862
Merrimack, NH 03054

The first volume of Lessons by Alex is available at
amazon.com, barnesandnoble.com and at all other
online and conventional bookstores.

If you do not see it on the shelves, ask them to
order it for you.

Distributed worldwide through Ingram Book Group

Printed in the United States
76475LV00003B/178-186